PLANNING PROGRAMS FOR EARLY EDUCATION OF THE HANDICAPPED

PLANNING PROGRAMS FOR EARLY EDUCATION OF THE HANDICAPPED

edited by
Norman E. Ellis
and Lee Cross
in association with
Kennith W. Goin

Published by
WALKER AND COMPANY
720 Fifth Avenue
New York, NY 10019

for

The Technical Assistance Development System
A Division of Frank Porter Graham
Child Development Center at
The University of North Carolina, Chapel Hill

Acknowledgments

In addition to the authors, the editors, and the production staff, there are several persons whom we must acknowledge for their roles in transforming the presentations made at Tucson into this book. We are grateful to Tealey Collins for her help in organizing the publication; to Carolyn Mears for her assistance in editing the manuscripts; to Melvin G. Moore and Ginny Dickens for their help in preparing the rationale material, and to Barbara Pearce for typing the manuscript. It goes without saying, of course, that we are in the debt of all those people from the states who took part in the conference.

This book was developed pursuant to a grant from the United States Office of Education. Grantees who undertake such projects under government sponsorship are encouraged to express freely their judgment in professional and technical matters. Points of view or opinions do not, therefore, necessarily represent official Office of Education position or policy.

First published in the United States of America in 1977 by the Walker Publishing Company, Inc.

Published simultaneously in Canada by Fitzhenry & Whiteside, Limited, Toronto

ISBN: 0-8027-9039-9

Library of Congress Catalog Card Number: 76-42883

Printed in the United States of America

10 9 8 7 6 5 4 3 2 1

Contents

Foreword

This book is the result of a conference for state education agency personnel held in Tucson, Arizona in February of 1974. The emphasis of the conference was planning programs for young handicapped children. The contents of this book reflect the proceedings of the conference and focus on selected planning issues. The major issues included have relevance not only for state education agency staff, but for everyone involved in planning and implementing programs for young handicapped children.

The book is divided into four parts. Part I, "Planning Considerations," contains four chapters. Chapter 1, "General and Historical Rationale for Early Education of the Handicapped" by Samuel A. Kirk, offers a vivid historical account of the growth of early education for the handicapped. Dr. Kirk clearly describes the trends that have swayed the attitudes of governmental, health, and education professionals in developing programs for children with special needs. James J. Gallagher in Chapter 2, "Planning Programs for Children," discusses the history of governmental planning programs for education of the handicapped. He then offers an approach to planning. This approach, which is presented in the form of a model, includes the crucial components of any sound planning effort. "Planning: A Federal Perspective" by Robert Herman contains information on current federal legislation which will affect the provision of services to young handicapped children. It also contains information on the nature of the relationship that the Bureau of Education for the Handicapped hopes to foster between itself and the states. In Chapter 4, "Planning: A State Perspective," John Melcher addresses a major planning need: information. Specific information needs in Wisconsin are addressed.

Part II, "Program Alternatives," includes chapters which address the topic of program alternatives at the state education agency level. In Chapter

5, Norman E. Ellis provides a conceptual definition of "program" and examines the factors (e.g., legislation) that affect alternatives. Some of the problems that plague agencies as they begin to formulate the programs they will use in providing services for children are explored. The next three chapters concern specific programs in Washington, Virginia, and New Jersey. In these papers, the various factors that had to be considered in developing particular parts of the states' early childhood plans are discussed. Wayne Spence describes the geographical and interagency problems that the Washington plan had to solve; Wayne B. Largent discusses the legislative conditions and the "child's age" alternative that the Virginia plan was led to consider; and Tealey L. Collins describes the parent training alternative in New Jersey's plan.

Part III, "Planning Comprehensive Services," addresses one of the most persistent and difficult questions confronting state special education agencies: "What constitutes comprehensive services at the state education level?" This question involves two issues: (1) What is the best range of services? and (2) What framework or procedures can be used to organize the existing range of services at the state level? Chapter 9, "Identifying and Planning Services for Children" by David L. Lillie, addresses the question: "What are comprehensive services?" Dr. Lillie provides a conceptual framework, in the form of a matrix, to help planners graphically organize existing services in their states. The matrix also allows the user to identify gaps in the services provided in his state or region. In Chapter 10, "Using a Matrix in Identifying Services," Anne L. Connolly and Ruth Ann Rasbold report on the use of Dr. Lillie's matrix in Massachusetts. The chapter shows how specific dimensions of the matrix must sometimes be modified in order to be used in a given state. The presentation also includes specific information on conditions in Massachusetts, in areas such as legislation, which necessitated modification of the instrument.

Part IV, "Identification Services," was included in this book because a large number of states are currently involved in developing and implementing "child-find" plans. In Chapter 11, "Identification of Young Children with Handicaps: An Overview," Lee Cross defines casefinding, screening, diagnosis, and assessment and explains the relationship of each service to the others. Chapter 12, "Considerations for Screening," is designed to familiarize the reader with the principles and practice of screening. After a brief section on the history of screening, William K. Frankenburg offers a concise definition of the term which is followed by discussions of "how to select conditions to screen for" and "what criteria to use in selecting screening procedures."

Appendix A, "Legislation for Handicapped Children," provides the reader with an overview of federal legislation that may be a source of funding for providing services to young handicapped children. Appendix B, "Developing a Rationale for Early Education,"focuses on the most pertinent literature on the development of early intervention services for young handicapped children.

PART ONE

PLANNING CONSIDERATIONS

CHAPTER 1

General and Historical Rationale for Early Education of the Handicapped

Samuel A. Kirk

In the history of early education in this country, practically everything on the development of intelligence has been confined experimentally and theoretically to the relationship between genetics and/or environment. I call this concern the "nature-nurture" controversy. People doing work in the field of the deaf and blind have had little difficulty convincing others that early education of a deaf child is necessary to produce speech or that such education is necessary to promote the earlier development of a blind child. It has been a little difficult, however, to convince people that early education is important for other children too. There has been resistance to early education in some instances because people felt a young child should be at home with his mother. It was considered the responsibility of the family to mold the child during his early years; in many places, consequently, there has been great resistance even to kindergarten.

The Nature-Nurture Controversy

The research literature in early education (see Appendix B) has primarily been confined to the controversy about the development of intelligence. Twenty years ago I read a book that hypothesized that political liberals believe in nurture (that environment influences intelligence), whereas political conservatives and geneticists believe in nature (that intelligence is fixed at birth). As proof for the thesis, case histories were cited from Darwin and many others who were either geneticists or environmentalists. The hypothesis was upheld by all these cases except one——the case of an individual who was a political liberal but a great believer in the constancy of the I.Q. and the inheritance of intelligence. Needless to say, this ruined the hypothesis.

Alfred Binet

The inventor of intelligence tests, Alfred Binet, was not a believer in the constancy of the I.Q. As a matter of fact, in 1911 he wrote a book that contained a chapter on the "educability of intelligence." That chapter is interesting for two reasons. First, Binet did not believe, as American psychologists did, in the fixed nature of the I.Q.; he believed in its alterability through training. Second, we know Alfred Binet today as the inventor of intelligence testing, but actually he constructed the test only to determine the characteristics of children for educational purposes. He was the one who started special classes for the mentally retarded in Paris in 1909 and 1910 in order to "educate" intelligence. In "The Prejudice Against the Educability of Intelligence," he wrote:

> I regret that I have often found a prejudice against the educability of intelligence. The familiar proverb that says "When one is stupid, it is for a long time," seems to be taken literally by non-critical teachers. [Teachers] are completely indifferent to the pupils who lack intelligence. They have neither sympathy nor even consideration for them, for their immoderate language in the presence of the children in this connection takes the following trend: "He is a child who will never do anything. He is poorly endowed. He is not at all intelligent." Too often have I heard these careless words. They are repeated every day in the elementary schools, and the secondary are not exempt from the charge. I remember that during my examination for the baccalaureate the examiner, Martha, irritated by one of my responses, declared that I would never have a philosophical mind. Never. What a strong word. Some modern philosophers seem to have given their support to this deplorable verdict by asserting that the intelligence of an individual is a fixed quantity which cannot be augmented. We must protest and react against the brutal pessimism. We shall try to demonstrate that it has no foundation.

That was written in 1909. We in early education have been repeating the same thing ever since; i.e., that we can ameliorate, that we can alter, that we can prevent further deterioration of mental function if we start young. To me, Binet is not only the father of intelligence testing, he is the father of "modern special education."

Harold Skeels

I became interested in this field when I was in Milwaukee in the 1930s. At that time I had had some experience with children whose I.Q.'s had been changed at an early age. In 1938, Harold Skeels came to Milwaukee to give a lecture to the social welfare department. He told them of his experience of taking children from an orphanage and placing them in an institution, thereby changing their I.Q.'s. After the lecture, Skeels came to my house for dinner. He gave me, that evening, a translated chapter of Binet's writings on the "educability of intelligence." That chapter was the only proof he had from the psychological literature that the I.Q. could be altered significantly. His story, I think, was fascinating. I should like to relate part of it here.

Skeels started out by going to an Iowa orphanage at the request of the Board of Control. There he found two one-year old babies that were not responding to their environment. Neither infant could do anything, and both looked like imbeciles. The Kuhlman Test of Mental Development was administered to them, and it was found that they had I.Q.'s of 46 and 35. An institution for mentally retarded children of that age was not then available in Iowa. There was, however, an institution that admitted children at older ages. So rules were broken, and these two so-called "hopeless" babies were committed to that institution.

A year later, Skeels happened to be visiting this institution and went into a ward for mentally retarded girls. He found a little baby running around—a three-year old child, happy and bright-looking. He asked, "Where did this child come from?" The answer was, "That's the one you sent a year ago." Later he went to another ward and found another bright-looking three-year old running around and receiving tremendous amounts of attention from older mentally retarded girls. Each child was tested again with the Kuhlman Test, and their I.Q.'s were found to be in the 80s and 90s. A year later Skeels tested them again, found them normal, and had them paroled to foster homes.

From this experience came the idea to start an experiment of taking babies out of the orphanage, putting them in institutions for the mentally retarded, and urging the older mentally retarded girls in the wards to give them a lot of attention. Skeels went to the Chairman of the Board of Control who was not a psychologist or a social worker but a corn farmer (and thereby probably more sympathetic to Skeels' views than professionals of that time). The Chairman listened to Skeels patiently as he told about the two children who had been paroled. The Chairman was sympathetic to the idea and approved the experiment.

After testing a group of twenty-five children in the orphanage with whatever infant tests he could find, Skeels selected thirteen children who were supposedly low in I.Q. and also had low ratings by the nurses, and took them to the institution. A year and a half later he retested them and obtained sensational results. The children he had taken to the institution for mental defectives had gained 28.5 points, and the twelve children he left in the orphanage had dropped 26.2 points. He had the temerity to report the results in the *Journal of Mental Deficiency* in 1939.

When the article appeared, the wrath of God fell on Skeels. Critics said the data was faked. Goodenough made a speech at the Academy of Science in which he said that, according to Skeels and Skodak, the thing to do is to take little babies and put them in an institution with feebleminded girls since, according to Skeels, the "girls can raise them better than we can." Skeels succeeded in retesting the children after they had been placed in foster homes and found that their accelerated I.Q.'s had been maintained. But by that time he was in disrepute as a psychologist and as an individual. He became discouraged with the proposition, left Iowa, and took a job in Washington working with the Public Health Service. We didn't hear from Skeels about this problem and the raising of I.Q.'s for many years. The controversy ceased because we all became involved in World War II.

The Bernadine Schmidt Study

In 1946, I read a number of articles published in the *Reader's Digest, The Ladies Home Journal,* and in a psychological monograph, which intimated that feeblemindedness could be cured. These articles were summaries of a doctor's dissertation at Northwestern University by Bernadine Schmidt. Since I was in Urbana (near Chicago), I decided to inquire about the research. My inquiry was met by an invitation to investigate all the relevant materials personally. I received permission from the Superintendent of the Chicago Schools to go into any file and to interview anyone that I wanted to in my efforts to ferret out the truth of the report. My investigation of the experiment was published in the *Psychological Bulletin* in July 1948. My article stated that the results of the research were not exactly what had been reported. Actually, what Bernadine Schmidt had done was to take adolescent children who received I.Q. scores of 40-45 on an Otis Quick Scoring Test and make the I.Q.'s normal. Because the report discredited the results of the study, it was welcomed by psychologists.

The Kirk Experiment

In 1948, I was able to obtain a grant from the Institute of Mental Health. The Institute, which was only two or three years old, was not particularly interested in education. I was told that the pediatricians on the Board were rather intrigued that somebody would work with mentally retarded children. Some of the pediatricians, I was told, backed the work while others said that it was not a medical problem. It was very hard at that time to be awarded a federal grant because there simply weren't that many. Nonetheless I was awarded what I think was one of the first non-medical grants from the Institute of Mental Health. The arguments and rationale for my study were largely what we have today: if we can elevate the mental and social abilities of children at a young age, we will prevent a lot of mental retardation.

The major purpose of the experiment in 1949 was to replicate Skeels' study in an institution and in a community with three-, four-, and five-year old mentally retarded children. The experiment was conducted in a state institution with a population of mental defectives of 5,200. We selected fifteen children, ages three to five, whose tested I.Q.'s were between 40 and 60. We also selected fifteen children of the same ages and I.Q.'s who would not receive training but would be tested periodically. We trained the experimental group for two years.

Figure 1 shows the development of the children in the experimental group at age eight, two years after they left the preschool. The graph shows that the trained group accelerated in mental and social maturity while the control group, like Skeels' control group, dropped on all tests. Although the increases and decreases in I.Q. were significant, what really meant something was that, out of the fifteen children, seven increased in I.Q. and behavior enough to be paroled from the institution. Those seven children went back to their homes or to foster homes. I understand from a follow-up study that, out of the seven paroled, six remained in the community four years later; while of the control group not a single one had been paroled from the institution four years later. In fact, the children in the control group were more mentally retarded psychometrically at age eight than they had been at age six. Our experimental group did not make the increases in I.Q. made by the Skeels children, probably because one-half had a definite medical diagnosis of pathology whereas none of Skeels' children had such a diagnosis.

In a second experiment in the community, we compared a group of children who attended the preschool to their twins or siblings who did not attend. This experiment was an attempt to control the home factor with the dependent variable being preschool attendance. I designed the experiment originally for twins; one twin of each set was to attend the preschool while the other was to remain at home. But nature did not provide me with more than two sets of twins. I settled for taking siblings a year or two apart.

Figure 2 compares the progress of children who were given preschool education with the progress of their twins or siblings who remained at home during the preschool years, but who were tested at the age of eight after being in school two years.

Four of the children were taken out of their inadequate homes and placed in foster homes and in preschool; these children made the most progress. Twelve of the children remained in their psychosocially inadequate homes and attended preschool; these children showed significant improvement (yet less than the foster home children). The sixteen twin and sibling control children, who were not enrolled in the preschool but who attended regular school until the age of eight, dropped in their rates of mental and social development.

The conclusion we drew from this experiment was that intervention at the preschool level accelerates the rate of mental and social development, while no intervention at that age level tends to allow the rate of mental and social development to slow. While the inferential statistics used in this study showed group results, the most important findings, as far as I was concerned, were to be derived from intensive study of the individual cases.

FIGURE 1

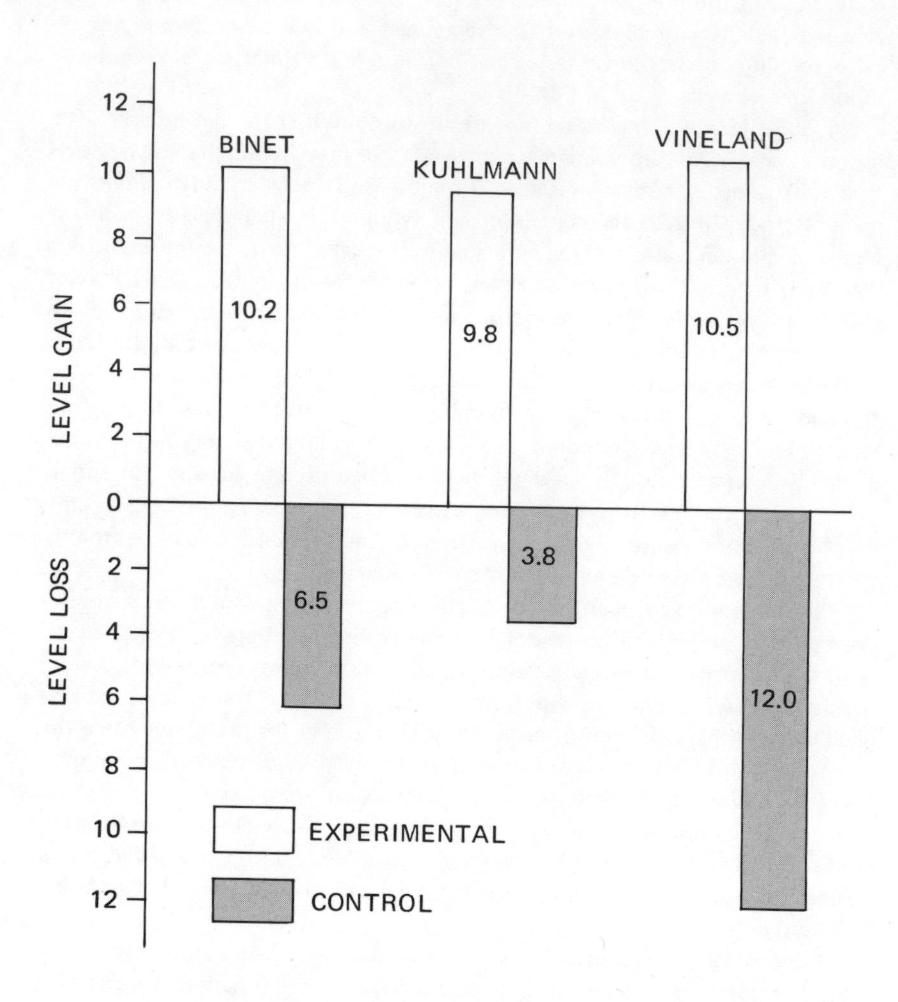

FIGURE 1: I.Q. and S.Q. change scores of institutionalized retarded children as a function of preschool experience.

Kirk, S.A., The education of intelligence. The Slow Learning Child, July, 1973, 20, 69.

FIGURE 2

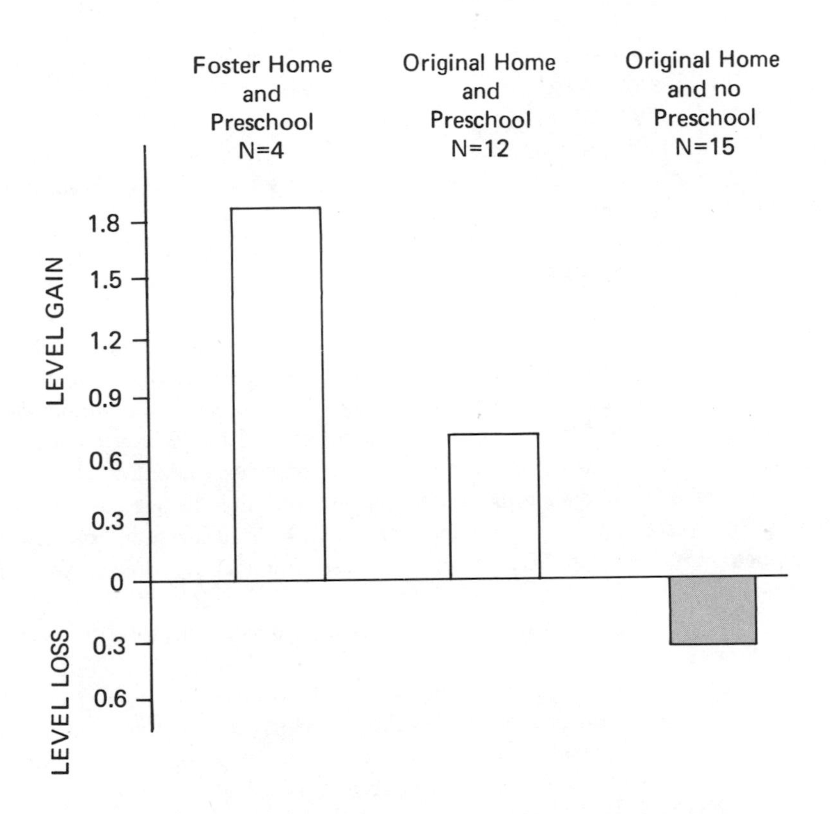

FIGURE 2: Average change in levels of development as a function of preschool and foster home experience.

Kirk, S.A., The education of intelligence. The Slow Learning Child, July, 1973, 20, 71.

For example, one of the four-year old boys was committed to the institution at the age of two and one-half on the grounds that he was feebleminded and had convulsive disorders. When admitted to the preschool at age four, he showed no convulsive disorders although his EEG was abnormal. He could not talk; he could only babble unintelligibly. His I.Q. scores on the Binet, Kuhlman, and Minnesota Preschool tests ranged from 50 to 60. In the preschool, he developed rapidly, and on successive tests administered every six months, he scored 75, then 85, and then 95. At the time of the third test, he was nearly six years old, and was paroled to Champaign-Urbana where he was placed in our community preschool. He was later adopted by a family and placed in the first grade. He had difficulty in learning to read although his I.Q. was then about 104. He was tutored, learned to read, and progressed satisfactorily until the fourth grade, which he repeated. From then on, he progressed year by year, through grade school, high school, and eventually college. He is now a teacher.

There was another boy in the institution who made similar progress. He was four years old, the youngest of a family of five children, all of whom were committed to the institution. The other children had I.Q.'s of about 70. His mother was an alcoholic, and his father was mentally defective. The child developed rapidly in the preschool; he did so well that he was paroled and placed in a foster home. Two years later, when he was seven and one-half, I examined him. With an I.Q. of 108, he was doing above average work in reading, writing, and arithmetic in the second grade. He was adopted, and since then I have been unable to find him; adoption agencies destroy the records after adoption.

One of the boys in the community school offered us an opportunity to study a child under environmental conditions which were different from the cases previously described. This boy tested at a 70 to 80 point I.Q. when he was admitted to the preschool at age four. We had difficulty helping him adjust or improve. He seemed to be disturbed every morning because of the treatment given him by his emotionally disturbed mother. The teacher reported: "There's more to this boy. He's always a little bit disturbed because of what happens to him at home." We asked the social agencies to remove him from his home, but they were unable to obtain the mother's permission. One day they committed the mother to a mental hospital and, consequently, had to find a foster home for the boy. At this time he was six years old, had improved very little in our preschool, and appeared to be inattentive and disturbed. They placed him "in a farm home" and in the first grade. After a year in the home (while he was in the second grade) we tested him; we found a stable boy doing good second grade work in reading, writing, and arithmetic. His I.Q. was over 100.

It was while he was in second grade that tranquilizers were coming into prominence. The boy's mother was placed on the medication and allowed to go home. She then requested that her son be returned to her. After two years with his mother, we tested him again (age ten) and found that his I.Q. had dropped back to 75. His academic achievement was still at a second grade level, and his appearance and mannerisms indicated that he had returned to his previous nervous state. This child's I.Q., behavior, and personality changed with the change in environment. In other words, the psychometric tests demonstrated that his educational achievements accelerated in a normal environment and decelerated in an abnormal environment.

The Heber Experiment

Rick Heber criticized my study by saying that I did not start young enough with the children. He was interested in starting at birth with high risk children. He began an experiment six or seven years ago with fifty pregnant women from high risk areas in Milwaukee. He divided the fifty women into an experimental group and a control group. For the experimental group, he sent teachers to the homes after the children were born. When these children were four months old, he transported them to a school where he has been educating them for the last six years. Figure 3 shows the results of yearly tests on the two groups over a six-year period. You will note from this graph that the two groups were about the same at age twelve months but that the experimental children soon surpassed the control group. At the six-year level, the experimental group had a mean I.Q. of 122 while the control group's mean I.Q. was at the 90-point level. Although Dr. Heber has not reported his final results, I feel that this longitudinal study is more crucial than most of our studies. If it's done properly and reported accurately, it probably will be the definitive experiment on the training of children from birth.

The Skeels Follow-up

After my experiment was completed, someone urged Harold Skeels to follow-up the children he had reported on in 1939. Skeels agreed. He conducted his follow-up study, not by mail but by going back to Iowa to try to find out where the children lived or where someone who knew something about them could be found. After all, he had been out of touch with them for twenty-one years. The task was not easy. He told me that he went from door to door in Iowa, Florida, and Arizona just to find one person. Ultimately, he succeeded in locating the twelve children from the experimental group and the thirteen children that had remained in an orphanage. In 1966, he published a monograph which contained a report on these twenty-five children.

He found that all thirteen children in the experimental group were self-supporting and none was a ward of an institution. Of the twelve control children one had died in adolescence, and four were wards of institutions. Educationally, the two groups were quite divergent. The median grade completed by children in the experimental group was twelfth grade, while the median grade completed by children in the control group was third grade. This

FIGURE 3

MEAN I.Q. PERFORMANCE WITH INCREASING AGE
FOR THE EXPERIMENTAL AND CONTROL GROUPS

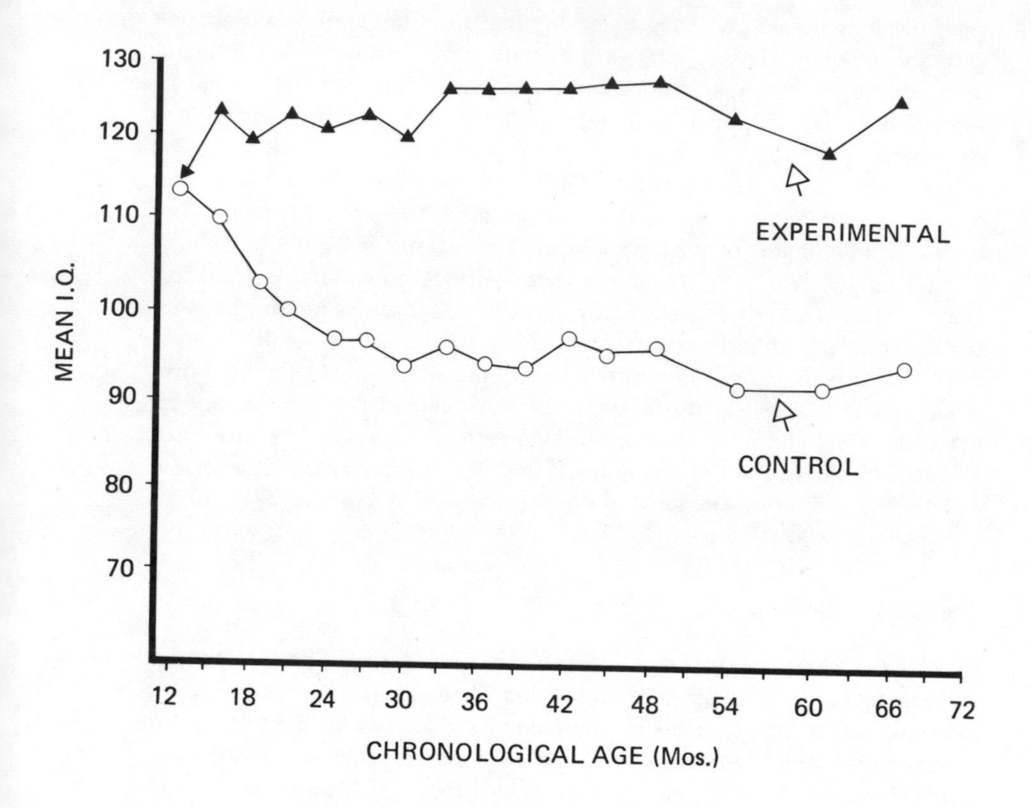

Kirk, S.A., The education of intelligence. The Slow Learning Child, July, 1973, 20, 74.

follow-up by Skeels after twenty-one years is one of the few longitudinal studies of early intervention that have been made, and it clearly demonstrates the long term effects of such intervention.

Federal Programs

It is difficult to trace the effects of these studies on later programs. For example, a number of years after the studies were completed (1964), Sargent Shriver became Director of Economic Opportunity. He was well acquainted with the results of the Skeels' study and also with my study on early intervention. He invited Skeels and me to his home to talk with him about the results of our research. Shortly after, and upon the advice of others, Shriver launched Head Start which, I think everyone agrees, is one of the most successful of the War on Poverty programs. The research that I have cited in this presentation was reported to Congress in 1968; the report helped a great deal in establishing the present early childhood program. The National Advisory Committee for the Handicapped, of which I was privileged to be Chairman, delineated for Congress the programs that should receive attention. We recommended immediate programs for preschool education of handicapped children, children with learning disabilities, inner-city children, and rural children. Two of these programs passed Congress; of the two, the bill for preschool education of the handicapped got the most attention. Having testified at the hearings for this bill, I can report that it was an easy bill to pass and actually the only education bill to pass in 1968, in spite of President Johnson's request that Congress not pass any new bills. I think the bill was not difficult to sell to Congress because we presented them with the results of research. Representative Qui made a statement to the effect that, from the evidence, the effectiveness of early intervention has been recognized for twenty years—let's not wait another twenty years before we implement it as a nation.

Concluding Statement

I don't think we ought to go overboard on the nature-nurture issue. I think all agree that intelligence is inherited, but I don't think that is the point. The geneticist Dobzhanski has stated that we are born with (what he called) a "norm of reaction" or a "reaction range." We do not know what the reaction range is in a particular individual, since people differ in their inheritance of reaction ranges. I interpret these ideas to mean the following: I may be born with an I.Q. of 75-100; if I have poor early environment it will be 75; if I have maximum opportunities it will be 100. We cannot create miracles with environmental changes, but we can contribute to each individual's development within his own reaction range.

From the point of view of historical rationale, I think we can say that we have some evidence that we can improve the functioning of children when we start intervention at an early age. Furthermore, neglect of adequate intervention is liable to inhibit the child's development. I think that if we have universal preschool education for all children, we will prevent functional retardation. The Russians obviously have strong feelings on this matter; they, being Lamarckians, believe in the effects of early training on development. They begin preschool education as early as six months of age. So do many of the countries in Europe. From an economical point of view, an ounce of prevention is worth a pound of cure. Prevention, economics, and humanism are all on the side of expanding preschool education. I hope that we will eventually arrive at expansion as a national goal.

BIBLIOGRAPHY

Binet, A. *Les idees modernes sur les enfants.* Paris, 1911.

Kirk, S.A. An evaluation of the study by B.D. Schmidt entitled: "Changes in personal, social, and intellectual behavior of children originally classified as feeble minded." *Psychological Bulletin,* July, 1948, *45* (4).

Kirk, S.A. The education of intelligence. *The Slow Learning Child,* July, 1973, *20.*

Schmidt, B.D. Changes in personal, social, and intellectual behavior of children originally classified as feeble minded. *Psychological Monographs,* 1946, *60,* (5), pp. 1-144.

Skeels, H.M., and Dye, H.B. A study of the effects of differential stimulation on mentally retarded children. *Proceedings and Addresses of the 63rd Annual Session of the American Association of Mental Deficiency, 44* (1), pp. 114-130.

CHAPTER 2

Planning Programs for Children

James J. Gallagher

Planning is an important tool for improving the services that we deliver to handicapped children. The plan that each state is asked to devise for serving its handicapped youngsters has the potential of significantly increasing the amount and quality of present services. In this paper, three major topics which should prove useful to early education planners are addressed: (1) the history of planning in current education, (2) the categories of information that a planning model forces its user to consider, and (3) the problems currently faced in planning efforts.

History of Planning

Certainly one of the startling changes that has taken place in education in America has been our attitude toward program planning. It's easy to forget how we felt, as a society, about planning ten or fifteen years ago. Planning had a slightly foreign taint to it. It was almost un-American. The American way was to stumble through things and to come out at the other end on top. America, it has been said, is the only nation that raised "ad hocism," as a desirable way to meet problems, to a level of national policy. The fact that we have survived a couple of world wars without really preparing for them very much and that we have gone through a number of other crises has led us to think that America could do anything it wanted, anytime it wanted, as long as the country got its whole heart and soul into the problem. You've got a problem like polio? Fine. We'll just put a lot of resources into it and we'll solve the problem. We've had enough success with this kind of ad hoc, let's-play-it-as-we-go kind of strategy to encourage us to believe that we were invulnerable against the ravages of time or ugly surprises.

I think now we see the mortality of our national society more clearly. The popularity of program planning is in fact linked to the loss of self-confidence and to the belief that our abilities and resources are unlimited. We've had the experience of Vietnam and the energy crisis which make it clear that our resources are not unlimited and that there will not always necessarily be a happy ending to all of the things that engage our attention. The acceptance of our limits leads to the notion that we must conserve systematically. We must apply our limited resources to those problems that are most important to us.

In addition to the realization that we as a nation have limits, the sizeable doubts about education's ability to carry out what it says it is going to do will force us to accept program planning. The general public feels that we promised to do certain kinds of things for disadvantaged children and that we didn't do them, or we didn't do them nearly as much as the public policy makers promised.

With the infusion of federal money, people began to realize that education was fully capable of spending great amounts of money, and that many times the money seemed to disappear without a trace. The public decision makers, the state legislators, the congressmen, the influential executive department people began to say: "Let's order our priorities. Let's maximize these resources. We cannot continue to just open the treasury and pour out more money into education or, for that matter, into anything else. So we must review what we are doing. We must show that we are trying to improve or eliminate unworthy efforts."

A Planning Model

There are a number of planning models available, each of which has its own strengths and weaknesses. However, four or five major components are contained in every planning model. Figure 1 shows such a model.

One of the things that any model is going to ask you to do is to get some notion of *needs,* needs that automatically lead you to a statement of *goals,* and goals that lead you to more specific statements of what you can reasonably expect to accomplish, i.e., *objectives.* Given your resources and constraints, in terms of items like funds and personnel, you have to decide on the kind of *alternative program directions* or strategies you're going to consider. So you need a set of criteria that will allow you to choose the alternative that best fits your needs under your circumstances. After making the choice, you have the problem of implementing the alternative and then of making a judgment. Did your choice help you accomplish what you set out to do in the first place? With the *feedback* gained by using the model, you have valuable assistance in making future decisions which affect your resources, objectives, and goals.

FIGURE 1

PROGRAM PLANNING AND EVALUATION MODEL

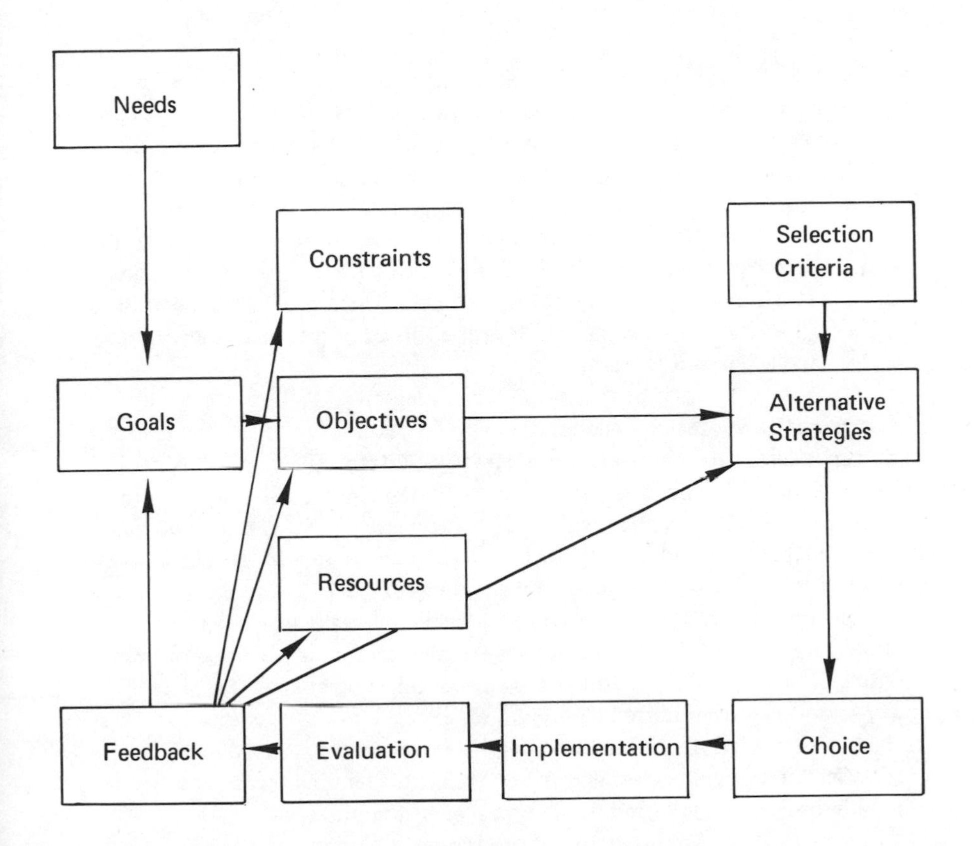

REPRINTED FROM:

Gallagher, J., Surles, R., & Hayes, A. Program planning and evaluation. Chapel Hill, North Carolina: Technical Assistance Development System, The University of North Carolina, 1973.

Planning Areas

Many people have devised various models. Upon careful examination of their major elements, however, it will be found that the models contain the same basic components: the components shown in Figure 1. So instead of talking first about models, let me point out what a planning system with these components makes us do that we don't normally do in our decision making.

Problem Definition. First, planning makes us define the scope of the problem by forcing us to collect data on the problem's size and nature. How many preschool handicapped children are there? What kinds of handicaps do they have? What are their major needs? Sensible planning demands that these kinds of questions be answered, as well as possible, when planning begins from the baseline. Usually we can start programs without really worrying about the problem's scope if our concerns are of a limited nature: e.g., a few programs in a single community. When our concerns are of a broader nature (e.g., a state), however, it is easy to lose the thread of just how many youngsters are involved unless we define scope.

Alternative Strategies. Second, planning forces us to consider the identification of alternative strategies. These strategies often involve making projections on a multi-year basis. In education, we often start to use one or more of the particular strategies that deal with a problem before we start to plan. We're not sitting around waiting for planners to come up with answers. There are kids out there who need help, and we have started to try to do something about helping them. Of course, nobody does planning the way the model suggests. As a matter of fact, most people are already in the business of implementing a strategy long before considering other strategies. For example, many states may have started a program of special classes for emotionally disturbed children; maybe that's the most effective strategy for educational remediation for the youngsters and maybe it isn't. Planning forces you to consider alternative strategies and weigh one against the other.

It's particularly important for those who are planning in the area of preschool education to identify and consider viable alternatives. We haven't yet committed the various professions (education, medicine, etc.) to a single well-accepted delivery system for preschool youngsters. Because we are really not locked into particular ways of dealing with the problems, we have options. We still have time in special education to think about what we would really like to do.

Choice. Third, a planning system forces us to consider the implication of various strategies and to develop the criteria needed to choose the best strategy. To establish the criteria, we must be aware of the available resources for each of the strategies; resources mean not just money, but personnel. For example, you might say that every child needs to have his or her own psychiatrist to deal with his or her own emotional problems. That isn't going to work because there aren't that many psychiatrists around. When dealing with a local issue at a local level, you may misjudge the feasibility of a strategy. You can have a couple of psychiatrists, and you may be able to run an interesting program to serve the needs of some handicapped children. But you will be able to serve only a certain percentage of children with a particular need before you have to switch strategies because you've run out of your special resources——for example, psychiatrists.

What we've hidden from ourselves is that a program alternative that can work very well in serving 20 percent of the handicapped group may not work at all in serving 100 percent. So, we have to determine what percentage of the handicapped group we really want to serve. If we commit ourselves to 60 or 90 percent, some of the strategies that could work very well in serving 20 percent are not going to work for us. Defining criteria in this way and considering what it will cost in manpower and money to extend a particular program to a regional level or to a state level is very useful. It makes us stop and realize that some program alternatives which look good will not work.

Let me give you a fair example of how to consider alternatives. Say that you want to provide programs for the gifted. How many children are there in the United States? Let's say that there are around fifty million children between the ages of five and seventeen. If you figure that two percent of these youngsters are gifted, then you have roughly a million children to serve. Let's say that one strategy to serve these children is to develop a masters-degree-plus-training program for teachers who are specialists in curriculum and in particular strategies for working with gifted children. These teachers, after training, will work with other teachers to help develop skills. (This is a commonly accepted strategy.) For every one supervisor (masters-degree-plus teacher), you can provide service to 200 children. What does that mean then? It means you need 5,000 supervisors. How much is needed in order to get 5,000 supervisors? Fifty universities will, for ten years, have to turn out ten masters-plus students per university per year. Simple arithmetic. What's interesting about all of this is that there isn't one university in this country even approaching this kind of training program! You obviously are not going to get fifty universities to implement this advanced degree program. You are not going to get the money to train the teachers, and even if you had the money, where would the resources be in the universities to carry out the accepted plan? In other words, the strategy is not going to work. It might work for Cleveland, Ohio, but it won't work for the whole state of Ohio. It might work for a particular community in Illinois, but it is not going to work for the whole state of Illinois, and it's certainly not going to work for the whole country. You can go ahead and implement the strategy and you will deliver some services, but you will not be able to meet the needs of all the youngsters that you say you want to help.

So, the planning model, at this point, has forced you to think of other ways of achieving your goal. States are going to have to consider problems that we in special education have been able to put away unresolved in the back of our minds. The minute a state education agency begins to define its needs, then it has to say what kinds of strategies can reasonably be used to approach the needs without making the agency look silly or ridiculous when it seeks resources from the legislature.

Support Services. The ad hoc or crisis planning approach causes us to put aside one of the most important areas of program planning: i.e., the need for support services that back up the service delivery program. A service program often goes into effect as soon as money is available because there are people out there who need help. You have been wanting resources and money for a long, long time and when it finally comes, you say, "Good. Get it out there and let it help some people."

That is a humanistic but very inefficient strategy. Unless you are planning to build up your training and development resources or your technical assistance or outreach resources, you are going to have a large group of expanded service programs of dubious quality, and there will be little hope for improvement in the services the next year. One of the most advantageous aspects of planning is that it makes you ask, "What are the resources needed to get the job done well?" Then you are forced to ask, "Where are all these new training programs going to come from? Who is going to staff them? How are they going to be run? How are they going to be funded?" Because reasonably well-trained personnel are needed in the programs, you must plan for preparing teachers; you must answer the question, "Who's going to train?" and "Who's going to pay for training?"

Often these questions are put aside as if they were someone else's responsibility; sometimes they are put aside with a vague hope that *somebody* will take care of them. It's interesting that even the people who know best about these situations still fool themselves. I recall in my government service that when we would come up against a problem, five or six of us would sit around a table and ask, "Who's doing this kind of thing?" Maybe it was the development of new curriculum materials. "Well, I can't think of anybody offhand," we would continue, "but there must be somebody out there doing something like this."

One day we just said, "Now wait a minute. We've had enough of this talk. Maybe someone is and maybe someone isn't. Let's go down the states one by one. Is anybody in Maine doing anything, in New Hampshire, in Vermont?" We went across the country that way, and we ended by saying, "No. There isn't anybody doing that." We hoped or assumed that someone was doing what we needed, but the assumption was false.

I think that many of us in the service business tend to think that what we need has been done or is being done by the people in research and development. We say, "Surely in some laboratory or exciting experimental school someone is developing curriculum materials or sequential program activities that will be applicable to the needs of preschool deaf children or blind children or learning disability children." Maybe, but it's unlikely. At the Frank Porter Graham Center, for instance, we've been trying to hire somebody for about a year in a position that I think is one of the most exciting we have. We are looking for someone, with a firm theoretical grounding but also with practical experience with children, to organize sequenced instructional materials in a way that is effective for dealing with children from age three months forward. Try to hire somebody with those qualifications sometime. You may say, "We will go to where such curriculums are being developed." I can tell you that there are only about three or four places in this country where long-term, longitudinal curriculum efforts are being engaged in. If you can think of more, I would like to hear from you.

In short, it's dangerous to assume in planning that materials or people are available. It is better to assume that if you don't provide the resources at the state or the federal level, then the materials or resources will never be available. You're going to have a lot of service programs with which you're going to be disappointed because the people running them don't know how to develop particular materials or work with particular procedures. There's no reason why they should. You're asking too much if you expect such expertise from them.

If, in fact, we are going to have new ideas and new procedures that will make the next generation of special educators more proficient than the last, we have to plan for certain support services now. Before substantial training money became available to provide support resources in the areas of the visually and the auditorially handicapped, teacher training was conducted in the institutions that housed the affected youngsters; the training programs were the same from year to year. There really was little infusion of new ideas and new program activities. Tradition guided the instructional program for these children. Such was the cost of investing totally in service and not investing at all in training, research, and development.

Technical Assistance. Support services involve, in some instances, moving ideas and concepts from developers to practitioners. Technical assistance or outreach systems need to be organized to help in this delivery. Delivering involves, as the Technical Assistance Development System's staff well knows, complicated arrangements not easily devised. Suppose, for example, somebody at the University of Washington or Oregon discovered a really sensational way to identify and treat emotionally disturbed children or youngsters with learning disabilities. How long would it take for that idea and those practices to get to Tampa, Florida? Or Baton Rouge, Louisiana? Or Tucson, Arizona? How long would it take the new idea, even after it's validated, to get there? Can it be done merely by putting the new idea into university training programs? (Surely it should be put into university training programs if, in fact, it's valid.) If so, how long will it take to replace all of the teachers already in the field who are using the old outmoded ideas if you proceed by making certain that every new person from university training programs has the new skills and new ideas? It could take a generation or more. Obviously, just changing the university training programs—–as hard as that is—–is not sufficient.

Since technical assistance is often delivered over a large geographic area, it makes sense to think about state planning as a device to bring technical assistance systems into being. A lot of the support services we have been describing are not available because of the national commitment to local control of education. In the final analysis, however, if education were really always controlled locally we would have very few great universities in this country. Local communities cannot alone create great universities. Anything which extends its influence over and beyond local boundaries cannot be locally controlled. Your training program, your research, your development, your technical assistance, or your communications must be organized at and be the responsibility of state level planning.

Evaluation. The final component of any planning model involves answering the question, "Have we done what we said we were going to do?" In other words, it involves determining whether we have approached the standard of performance that we established for ourselves. Evaluation is most difficult from a psychological standpoint for educators (or anybody else) to face, because the news that we get from evaluations is almost always bad. At best, the news is that we have done what we said we were going to do. Anything short of that becomes a problem to us, to our credibility. The public and the decision makers who are allocating resources, however, will not allow us to put off evaluation. Thus, we must attempt to collect a wide variety of data that will allow us to demonstrate that we have been accountable to our funding sources.

The absolute necessity for support services, and the difficulty in getting money for them, has led me to suggest a type of "set-aside" support funds. These funds would be a part of the total allocation of service money. Instead of arguing for research money in the abstract we can say to our funding source that any service program worth its salt has got to have support services as part of the total program. Choose a figure for these funds that can be defended: e.g., 15 percent added to the service funds allotted should be reserved for support service activities (for training, for research, for program development, and for technical assistance). Instead of trying to argue the merits of each support area separately, we must argue that we need to have money for all of these areas for the total effort to succeed.

Unless state decision makers grab hold of the reins (as they can do) by using a planning model, however, preschool programs for handicapped children will not be implemented in the way that we would like. Political realities and pressures within the educational establishment, rather than stated priorities, often determine the allocation of resources. A specific example of this phenomenon is the application of the old Title VI program, the formula grants program, to the states. When that program was originally put into federal handicapped legislation, a number of suggested directions and priorities for spending the money were listed. One of these––and these priorities came not only from federal bureaucrats but also from the accumulation of information from professionals in the field, from state department people––was early education for handicapped children.

Many states did begin or expand their preschool efforts with these funds, but they did not expand the efforts nearly as much as theoretically could have been anticipated. What happened? Why didn't the priorities that were clearly stated get translated into action? The political realities of a variety of clients and consumers already on the spot in professional education in school-age programs for the mentally retarded, in learning disability programs, and in programs for the sensory handicapped––put pressures on state leaders to invest more resources in their own area of interest.

They, of course, had needs in front of them to justify their request. They pressured decision makers to place much of the Title VI resources into expanding existing programs rather than into beginning new efforts in preschool education. The lesson is clear. If one of our priorities is preschool education, we must systematically plan to have that priority in the total state plan for the allocation of resources. To allow the educational-political process of various power groups pressuring decision makers to survive will not permit our goals to be reached. A visible and clear long-range plan is one of the best weapons that state decision makers have against political pressure.

Problems in Planning

The whole process of planning, from the educational standpoint, is less than a decade old. We've still got a lot to learn in terms of how to use this tool. For example, one of the weaknesses in the federal government and in most state governments has been the separation of planning from budgeting. Unless planning and budgeting are, to some extent, married, planning tends to become unrealistic and theoretical, and it loses the attention of practical program managers. I suspect that this statement is true at the community level or any other level where planning goes on. Dozens, even hundreds, of small decisions about reallocation of budget monies, changing budget requests, and modifying budget proposals that go to the legislature influence policy. Sometimes, there is no one who really understands the overall implications of these daily and weekly shifts in budget allocations.

A second major weakness in current planning models is that planners often forget that they are aides to decision makers, not decision makers themselves. Instead of providing alternative directions which policy makers can use to make decisions, planners often put their personal priorities into plans and thereby alienate the decision makers. Planners should always remember that *their* power and influence is merely a reflection of the decision maker's power and influence. Unless they have the support and full confidence of the decision makers, they will have no influence at all. The best way to lose confidence is to slip pet ideas into plans while decision makers are not looking. When the question "Where did that come from?" is asked, confidence has been lost in the program planner's motives.

Another major weakness in our planning is that we are unable (and we must face up to this as strongly and forthrightly as possible) to evaluate our programs effectively and to get a total portrait of them. Consequently, we underestimate the effectiveness or impact of programs because we have not described their outcomes completely enough. An achievement test to measure gains in reading scores for educable retarded children is hardly sufficient to delineate the complex self-image and subtle additudinal changes, the reshuffling of family values and interests, the attitudes of others in the community, or the shift in the attitude of the community itself that can take place as part of the impact of this kind of program. Probably more than anything else, we need to develop more sophisticated evaluation tools for measuring the subtle impact of our programs, the impact which is beyond the evident change in the children being served.

Conclusion

With all of these weaknesses and the pressures I described at the beginning of this presentation, it is clear that planning is not only one of the more useful tools that educational decision makers will have, but that it is a tool that will be used, for good or for ill, for a long time to come. The allocation of scarce resources to meet overwhelming needs is not a situation that is going to disappear; we must use planning to deal with that issue. The trick is not just to relax and enjoy planning's inevitability; the trick is to find ways to use planning to bring, if not ecstasy, at least a reasonable amount of satisfaction in our efforts.

CHAPTER 3

Planning: A Federal Perspective

Robert Herman

Four issues face those involved in planning state programs for the handicapped child: (1) the nature of present and pending legislation, (2) the states' relationships with the Bureau of Education for the Handicapped [BEH], (3) the development of a priority plan in each state, and (4) the future of early childhood efforts in this country. The success of the state planning efforts will depend, in part, upon what happens in each of these areas.

Present and Pending Legislation

The law is becoming more and more favorable for early education of handicapped children (see Appendix A). For example, Public Law 93-380, Sections 613 and 615, has stipulations for the following areas of state planning: setting timetables, developing plans for serving all children, ensuring due process, soliciting parent and public approval, and setting a date by which all children will be receiving services. Section 504 of the Rehabilitation Act requires that there be no discrimination against handicapped individuals, whatever the setting (e.g., employment, school). A new section of the Elementary-Secondary Education Act of 1974, Section 1, calls for the United States Office of Education to adopt a policy of free public education for every child in this country. These sections, plus the new Education for the Handicapped Amendments, make the present time ideal for state planning efforts.

The States and BEH

We at BEH feel that one of the best ways to facilitate planning within states is to provide technical assistance and support to the states to facilitate their coming together in a joint planning session. We are not suggesting that the states jointly develop plans, but rather that the people from each state work on their own plan (in cooperative arrangements with the federal government) in a planning setting which includes other states working on their plans.

We do not suggest interstate planning because it is difficult to join objectives across state lines. Interstate planning has been tried many times, and it really never seems to work for many reasons: the independence of states; the individual needs and responsibilities of states; and the involvement of legislative, financial, judicial and political-social considerations.

Certainly, it makes sense to develop a close state and federal relationship. It would be a mistake to forget, however, that it is the states who have the responsibilities for educating their children and that the constitutions of most states specify that responsibility. BEH looks upon its role in state planning for early education as being that of an active but junior partner. Even though the three pieces of legislation mentioned earlier do come together in a splendid array which adds substantial federal support to state programs for the handicapped, the federal government––no matter what happens––can at this time be only a junior partner in terms of responsibility for the education of the children. We do now, and will continue, to play an active role in bringing about compliance to the current federal statutes.

Priority Plan

With $22 million, it is hoped that BEH will be able to provide the resources necessary in a great many states to implement or aid in the implementation of these state plans. We call the amount of money needed to bring change "the critical mass." In Minnesota, which we will call the median state, $450,000 for early education may just be the critical mass needed to bring about the implementation of a state plan and expand early childhood education for handicapped children.

In addition to the state plan, we are requesting that each state develop a "priority plan" for specific projects or activities that meet the needs of the particular state. The state education agency should be responsible for coordinating the development of the plan and the priority listing, and it should form a committee of public and private agencies from across the state to work on the plan. Once completed, the plan will be considered by BEH and discussed by BEH and the state. The funding of early childhood education projects will be based on the state priority listing and the state plan.

The Future

The early childhood education program has come of age. The commitment that the program signifies is only a part of the federal government's total commitment to full services for every handicapped child in this country. This commitment, plus the fact that BEH foresees no conflicts or challenges which would upset its long-term relationships with the state departments of education, holds promise for early education planning in every state.

The new federal laws, along with the movement for civil rights for the handicapped in the states and in Washington, D.C., have made it clear that the advocates for education of all handicapped children have won their fights. They have won in part through a number of fortunate circumstances coming together simultaneously. For example, under the new Freedom of Information Act, any federally subsidized program that works with children must reveal, to anybody who asks, what it is doing for those children. This law has made it possible for a number of groups such as the Children's Defense Fund, the President's Committee for Civil Rights under the Law, parent groups, the Council for Exceptional Children, and others to pursue their interests in determining how the laws are being carried out. The groups are very concerned with the federal government's posture on the laws. You can be assured that we at BEH are urging and requiring compliance at all levels.

Even with all the legal and public support, there are, of course, difficulties facing the states. They are faced with the responsibility of, and the requirements for, developing the plans. They are faced with providing the resources required to serve the numbers of children that are going to have to be served by a certain date. They are faced with planning for physical facilities and personnel. We trust that the commitment of the people working to give handicapped children equal educational opportunities will prevent the potential for conflict (over the laws) between the federal and state governments from ever being developed.

New resources to the states will allow for some expansion of programs serving the unserved child and, of course, the preschool handicapped. Positive action on new legislation will create an even stronger federal role in the education of the handicapped. Senate Bill 6 (which became Public Law 94-142 in early 1976) is moving its way through both houses of Congress; its potential effect is so far-reaching that it warrants close observation.

Closing Thoughts

The step-by-step manner in which state planning is proceeding is good. The technical assistance provided by TADS, the validation and implementation of preschool programs all over the country, and our studies of the 150 demonstration and outreach early childhood programs will all be of help in state planning.

The early childhood program is one of the most orderly and progressive of all federal programs. Its success is largely due to the cooperation of state people, consultants, and other early childhood supporters across the country. To continue our success, we've got to think positively about what is to come.

CHAPTER 4

Planning: A State Perspective

John Melcher

What information does a state agency need? How do you get the information to the agency? These are questions that we in Wisconsin have begun to consider. Seven areas in which we have found particularly pressing needs include: (1) identifying children, (2) using existing services, (3) predicting the incidence of various handicaps, (4) delivering services, (5) using a home management system, (6) developing a system of interlocking directorships among various service and funding organizations, and (7) providing quality manpower for our service programs (training).

Identifying Children

We in special education need to refine the methods we use to identify children. In many instances, we give only lip service to identification while we concentrate on diagnosis and providing services. We have a law in Wisconsin that says that every physician, every social agency, anyone who has reason "to suspect" (notice that language) that a child has a handicapping condition must report it. Unfortunately, we're not flooded with reports, even though this law has been on the books for a year and a half. Why not? I think the biggest reason is that service providers aren't sure that such a report will cause something good to happen to their clients (parents, children, etc.). We have not really conveyed this message to the service people: "If you'll spill the beans to us, we'll see that your relationship with your client is in no way marred, tarnished, or subrogated by our behavior."

One of the things that has complicated our relationship with the service people is the confidentiality laws: the Buckley amendment. Physicians and others don't want to expose incomplete data. They say, "My diagnosis is not confirmed." In fact, they are saying, "Until I can place my professional integrity 100 percent behind this referral, I'm not going to make the referral." Part of the problem is parental. By requiring a service provider to report, you're changing the relationship between the social agency and the parent because you're involving a third party in what the parent thought was an intimate two-way transaction.

In addition to the confidentiality issue, there are costs in reporting. If nothing else, few cents for postage. If nothing else, figuring out stenographic time to write up a report that the physician or social worker can be proud of. We have made no provisions for covering such costs, even though making a decent referral will definitely cost the reporter some money.

There are many ways of approaching the child identification problem. Birth certificate reporting is one well established route. Most states in the union have some provision in their health laws that say congenital anomalies must be reported on the birth certificate. These laws are not always followed. In our state, for example, those reports must be sent to our agency immediately after the birth of the child. We're finding that some people don't report a diagnosis on the birth certificate because they're worried about marking a youngster for a long time, or they think the child's condition will be remedied by the time he or she goes to school.

Another way to find children is through the screening programs under Title XIX. To get referrals from non-school programs, however, you have to go over and ask the people, "What can we do together?" Another approach that is useful is the kindergarten round-up program. In most systems, by legislative mandate, each youngster must be thoroughly screened before entering kindergarten.

Using Existing Services

The use of existing services, especially medical, is important in a state agency effort. It is important in helping find cases, but it is also important in providing the best possible services to many people.

From the regional resource centers and the university affiliated programs to specialized clinics and the child sections of hospitals, you will find clients. You just need to spend time in a place such as Milwaukee Children's Hospital. There you will discover a ready-made population to serve. We must have some entree into places like Milwaukee Children's Hospital and the university hospitals where physicians from all over the state send their most complicated cases.

Our contacts in the area of non-public education have been very poor. At one time, a third of our elementary kids in Wisconsin were in parochial schools; now a quarter of them are in such schools. If we don't show the people running programs in these schools that we have something to offer financially that other programs can't offer, many children will go without service. As surprising as it may seem, if we don't develop a rapport with these people, their clientele will find it difficult to relate to us.

Head Start, nursery schools, Montessori centers, parent-run day care programs, hearing societies, speech clinics, and programs financed under the auspices of the Elementary and Secondary Act are all important to a statewide identification and service effort. If you have ever looked at the compilation of programs financed under Title I (ESEA) that concern preschool handicapped kids, you know the size of our task in finding and using existing services. How we relate or don't relate to the programs in the state is important. Our law, for example, says we will now supervise the programs in the state residential schools that are operated by health and social services. We have the same obligations to them as we have to others, even though we really know very little about that population. We used to be invited to the agencies every four or five years as friends. Now we have a different kind of obligation! If anything is wrong in state or county operated facilities, we are obliged to assume responsibility, just as we have been and must continue to be responsible for any public school program in the state of Wisconsin.

Predicting Incidence

We need measuring devices that are more accurate than those we now use in predicting the number of children requiring specific services. Moreover, we need devices which are attuned to cultural variations so that we do not misdiagnose children. The fact that our data on"the population to be served" has so often been inaccurate and contradictory has caused us to lose credibility with taxpayers and legislators. Why should early childhood programs be funded, the taxpayers ask, when the professionals' estimates of the number of children in the population needing services vary so greatly? The taxpayer is not shy anymore! He is not afraid to say "I want more data before you get anything. Let's get off the emotional level and get on with the facts." Or, he may even say, "I'm not so sure we want to spend money on these kids who have limited potential." Ten years ago, you didn't find many people like that.

Delivering Services

Just because you have a model in one of your state's major cities that works well, you cannot expect to transport the model to another locale without some difficulties. For example, there is an excellent program for children with cleft palates in Milwaukee. The program involves, however, up to six professionals working intensively with the children during the day. At night, the children are sent home to be with their specially trained mothers and dads. How do you bring the same level of services in Milwaukee to children in Florence or Forest County? Do you transport the children to the Milwaukee facilities? If so, what happens to the parent-child relationship?

I think we have to become more radical in our schemes for reaching out. For example, we could use helicopters to transport teachers or kids. We could use cassettes, for example, to orient blind parents. We must use the mails much more than we now do for all kinds of activities in early childhood. While looking for better methods of delivering the services now available, be careful not to make the mistake of considering one model as the ideal model for a whole state. Many models that can be applied in whole or in part in various situations are needed. Funding practices, consequently, should be equally supportive of all models.

Home Management Systems

When children are transferred from the programs formerly run by health and social services agencies to those run by communities, there are oftentimes problems. There must be some planning at the local as well as the state level if the children are to be received properly. For example, there are often logistical problems involved in providing services. Sometimes, clinic personnel show no respect for a child's or a family's time. The clinics force their clients to wait long hours because of inappropriate scheduling.

Most of the time, there are no counseling services for siblings and very few for parents. In my personal experience, many mixed up people have made terrible personal decisions because there was a handicapped member in the family, and they were worried about genetic, or personal, or other implications. We need to do even more for siblings than for parents because they are going to live longer, expectancy-wise. They are going to have their own sets of problems in an environment that the family may or may not have considered.

Transportation systems are another area that communities will have to consider when the children arrive. We have been most inefficient in transporting children. Have you ever looked at the costs of transportation per day? It's sometimes twenty-five, thirty, and thirty-five dollars.

Interlocking Directorships

As a state director in Wisconsin, I spent about a third of my time on other boards, e.g., on the Governor's Health Policy Board, on the State Developmental Disabilities Board, etc. I spent my time there for one major reason. I could learn. People often were suspicious of my presence, but I told them, "A lot of the action in our field involves different boards. We have to make contacts if we're going to provide the best services."

Training

We are at a point where we must decide what approaches we are going to have to use to be effective in preparing teachers for the new early education programs. Until now, we've often taken anyone who has had an announced interest and used them in programs such as day care. Some of the people in these programs have no theoretical training, but have an enormous amount of experience. How are we going to approach formal training for such people? Moreover, how are we going to train enough early childhood teachers for all the kids who are emotionally disturbed or who have a learning disability?

I think the answer to these questions is public support. If you've got the public with you (that public includes the legislature), money——even in tough times——is not the real problem because you are in the priority group. You don't get into the priority group by weeping for children or by staying inside. You have to run some risks and speak out.

You must fight for money for children. In the township in which my summer cottage is located, they just received a federal revenue-sharing grant. You know what they bought with it? School services? You've got to be kidding. They bought a road grader. What do they need more than a grader? Who wants to get stuck on a road in Northern Wisconsin? I'm certain you'll generally find——especially in poor states——that little revenue-sharing money is going into education. For that reason, it is important to start now in making contacts and garnering public favor.

Be pleasantly militant, get the facts, and then "sell" your plan to the "powers that be." Remember, what you're "selling" is the future of children in great need.

PART TWO

PROGRAM ALTERNATIVES

CHAPTER 5

Program Alternatives

Norman E. Ellis

There is general support for the notion that intelligent decision making involves weighing various alternatives. The purpose of this chapter is to provide a tool for considering program alternatives. Also presented in this chapter are a number of factors which may influence the choice of one alternative over others.

Definition

The tool provided in this chapter is a conceptual definition of program. A program is a set of activities with specified outcomes for a defined target. The three key terms in this definition are: activities, target, and outcomes. In other words, a program must be designed to affect a particular group (target), in a particular way (outcomes) through a particular set of actions (activities).

This definition can be a tool to make discussions about program alternatives more meaningful. A considerable amount of confusion arises because the targets, outcomes and activities of the programs being considered are unclear. Sometimes, when the term "program alternatives" is used, the reference point is a statewide system, i.e., a system that would deliver services to all handicapped children in a state. At other times, the reference point is a specific target group, e.g., strategies to deliver services to hearing-impaired infants. At other times, program alternatives are used to refer to strategies that deal with geographical areas, e.g., service delivery strategies for rural and remote areas. On other occasions, program alternatives are used in referring to the service delivery point, e.g., a teacher or project delivering services to fifteen or twenty children. On still other occasions, program alternatives are used to describe specific curricular packages or other types of instruments.

In each of the preceding examples, confusion about the kind of alternatives being discussed can be traced to a lack of clarity concerning targets, outcomes, and activities. For example, when discussing program alternatives for rural and remote areas, you should include the geographical area as part of the description of the target, e.g., three- to five-year old children in rural areas. Similarly, the discussion of curricular materials does not constitute a program alternative because neither the target nor the outcomes have been identified. When all three components are specified, it is possible to consider alternatives because the level at which the alternatives are being considered can easily be recognized, e.g., the local education agency level as opposed to the statewide level.

The definition can also be used as a tool for comparing various alternatives. In order to choose among programs, it is necessary to have a framework upon which various programs can be compared. The framework should highlight the crucial dimensions of the programs, and it should place the decision maker in a position to choose a program which contains the dimensions necessary to meet existing needs. The target, activity, and outcome components of the definition provide these necessary dimensions.

Without a clear understanding of target, outcome, and activity, it is not possible to make consistent, appropriate decisions about alternatives. For example, a parent training program may be either a training program for parents and other paraprofessionals, a program to help parents use a particular curriculum with their children, or both. Without a clear understanding of the target and the outcomes, it would not be possible to decide among the alternatives of "parent training programs."

It is possible to choose from among various programs on the basis of one, two, or all three components. One could choose a program because of the target if one assumes that the outcomes and activities are acceptable. A choice could be made on the basis of activities if the program alternatives had similar targets and outcomes. An alternative could also be selected on the basis of the outcomes. And, of course, an alternative could be chosen because it contained a different target, different activities, and different outcomes than the other programs.

Influencing Factors

There are an infinite number of factors which can influence the selection of program alternatives. These factors include everything from the attitudes of a local building principal to the contents of federal legislation. Seven factors (which were selected because they are particularly salient, exist in all states, and influence program alternatives at all levels of state decision making) are discussed in this chapter. They are: (1) legislation, (2) characteristics of the children, (3) range of program support, (4) interagency relationships, (5) agency roles and expectations, (6) resource requirements, and (7) agency agreement.

In the following discussion, each factor is presented in the form of a general question followed by sub-questions. The questions and the subsequent discussions are oriented toward an education agency; however, they concern issues which each agency involved in providing services to handicapped children must address.

1. How will legislation affect program alternatives?

   a. Does the legislation make you responsible for either specific services to a specific client group or generally accountable for an ill-defined client group?
   b. Does the legislation either mandate or suggest cooperation among agencies to deliver services to children?
   c. Does the legislation specify some program components to be delivered by agencies other than the education agency, e.g., identification and screening to be done by public health?

The general question about legislation and the three sub-questions touch a number of issues. Sub-question (a) raises the issue of what difference does it make if you have legislation that identifies a specific target group and specified services rather than legislation within which both the target group and services are ill-defined? There are both positive and negative consequences for either one of these conditions; the nature of your state probably determines whether the advantages outweigh the disadvantages. For example, on the one hand, legislation that specifies who the clients are, what they have a right to receive, and what you are responsible for delivering, will essentially legitimize and institutionalize your program. While, on the other hand, the same kind of legislation could make it difficult to have developmentally based programs for children because the legislation specifies categorical handicapping conditions.

Sub-questions (b) and (c) concern the division and coordination of services. Sub-question (b) is concerned with how the legislation deals with interagency relationships. Sub-question (c) raises the issue of the division of program components among agencies. Again, there are both positive and negative consequences whatever the nature of the legislation, and the consequences must be interpreted in terms of the conditions in each state. For example, in a state which has well defined, functional relationships among its agencies, it is probably sufficient if the legislation refers to interagency relationships in a general way. However, in other states, it may take a legislative mandate to get interagency cooperation.

Anne Connolly, in the following paragraphs, describes the impact of Massachusetts legislation. Her description highlights both the specific issues involved in interagency relationships and the general impact of legislation on a specific group, i.e., young handicapped children. In addition, Ms. Connolly addresses the implementation of non-categorical legislation, the development of regulations, the role of parents, and screening.

The Associate Commissioner for Special Education is presently in a meeting that is called the "Intersecretariat Meeting." This is an important meeting because our legislation––Chapter 766 of the Acts of 1972––requires that seven state agencies work cooperatively in promulgating regulations for children with special needs. The Intersecretariat Meeting, which is attended by the secretaries of human services (public health, mental health, youth services, welfare, and various related agencies) and education, is designed to help the agencies involved decide "who is responsible for what" and "who pays for what." This meeting is especially important because Chapter 766 of the Acts of 1972, the Comprehensive Special Education Law, mandates that local education agencies are responsible for the education of children from three to twenty-one. Although the law mandates cooperation among seven state agencies, the monies actually have remained in the same agencies in which they have always been. This is one of the biggest problems faced by the local education agencies. They feel very strongly that if they are responsible for all screening and identification, evaluation, and program planning some of the monies that are presently sitting in mental health, public health, and in youth services should be shared.

The Law. Chapter 766 which went into effect on September 1, 1974, states that mandatory education is for children at preschool age who have (and this is in the law) "substantial disabilities." Although education is not mandated below three in Massachusetts, school systems that choose to service this population are reimbursed. "Substantial disability" is a term used in the regulations to describe a special need in a child of ages three or four. We don't identify anybody with terms such as deaf, blind, or retarded in our legislation anymore. We rather refer to all target children as children with special needs. A school-age child with special needs is a child who has been identified by his CET (Core Evaluation Team). A CET is a group of professionals who evaluate a child and come up with an educational plan. Ideally, the plan defines what the child needs and how we're going to provide for those needs. Referrals must be based upon a finding that a school age child, because of temporary or more permanent adjustment difficulties or attributes arising from intellectual, sensory, emotional, or physical factors, cerebral disfunctions, perceptual factors or other specific learning disabilities or any combination thereof, is unable to progress effectively in a regular educational program and requires special education.

A child of age three or four, according to our legislation, is substantially disabled if the CET determines that there is a reasonable likelihood that when the child enters kindergarten he or she will have special needs as defined in the preceding paragraph. While the legislature has defined preschool (three to kindergarten) disability, we have decided that the Core Evaluation Team is responsible for evaluating each child who is referred and for deciding whether or not the child needs special services.

Background. Let me give you a little background on how our regulations came about. The law passed the legislature in July of 1972. The state division of special education at that time had about one-fourth the number of people that are presently working in the division. Quite a few people have been hired using federal funds, which is the only way that Massachusetts would have been able to even come close to dealing with a law as comprehensive as Chapter 766. The Associate Commissioner when the law passed the legislature, Dr. Joseph Rice, said, "How are we going to do this with no staff?" So they set up ten task forces which ended up being prototypes for some of the twelve chapters of our regulations. One of the task forces was the task force on preschool programs. We had people on this task force who were involved in preschool programs in the Department of Mental Health, people from public health, professors from the university, and teachers of early childhood education. All of these people were involved in a very long process of developing a report, a very long report––about forty-five pages.

Preschool Divisions. In our regulations, we have a whole chapter on the education of children from three to four (Chapter 6, "Services for Children, Ages Three to Four"). The people involved in early education are still not confident that Chapter 6 represents their needs. We have sections in the Chapter on identification of children with substantial disabilities; referral for evaluation of children with substantial disabilities; evaluation of children of ages three and four; educational planning; and parent involvement. It's interesting that we don't talk about parent involvement in early childhood education until we get to the development of an educational plan. That's one of the controversies between our early education people and the State Department of Education. Generally the results of the evaluation process, which is a comprehensive process of assessment, is an educational plan. Basically, the plan is a contract between a parent and the school system for the provision of necessary education for a particular child.

Screening for preschool children is mandated by the regulations, but it's optional on the part of the parent. That is, a school system must make every available effort to publicize preschool screening. Now, in Massachusetts, when school systems do the screening for kindergarten they often publicize the event in the newspaper: "We are holding free screening for any child from age three to kindergarten. Bring your children and we'll screen them; then we'll give you an educational plan after we evaluate them if it's necessary." The results of the advertisement are very different. With a mandate, the systems must advertise. How they advertise is their business. Some school systems do a lot of things. They use television, notes home with brothers and sisters, newspapers, church, and civic organizations. Then we have other school systems that put a notice in *The Globe,* which is our big newspaper, on page twenty-nine on the lower right-hand corner. Unfortunately, it is often communities that have a lot of children who need screening that use page twenty-nine of *The Globe* to wrap their message. We have not found that the screening process really gets to the population below kindergarten age at all.

Ms. Connolly could, no doubt, have touched many other issues in her discussion. Her description, however, provides excellent samples of the influence of legislation on program alternatives.

2. How will the characteristics of the children, e.g., age and degree of handicap, influence program alternatives?

The number of child-related characteristics which might influence alternatives is, of course, limited only by the nature of the agency's role (legislated or otherwise) in early education. The two most obvious characteristics are age and degree of handicap. The type of program alternatives and program requirements are different if the target group is infants as opposed to children six years of age. Similarly, programs for children who need only minor special education in many cases are not appropriate for children who need a great deal of help in many areas.

The geographical location and the cultural setting are two prominent influences on the selection of a program. Geographical location is the most obvious of the two. For example, a set of program alternatives which meets the needs of an urban population may have to be modified considerably before it can meet the needs of a rural, sparsely populated area. The cultural setting can influence program alternatives in a variety of ways. For example, parent programs are often conceptualized so that they deal with siblings. In few cases, however, have they been conceptualized in ways that deal with the extended family and other relevant social groups which have a tremendous impact on children.

3. Will your agency perform all of the following functions for any alternative: (a) assistance to programs, (b) regulations, (c) resource [funds] allocation?

    a. How will the three functions be balanced; e.g., will your agency primarily organize to regulate and allocate resources with a minor emphasis on assistance?
    b. How compatible are these three and other state agency functions?
    c. If some of the functions are incompatible, what are the consequences for program alternatives?

The three functions of regulating/monitoring, resource allocation, and assistance are essential features of almost any program alternative. The regulation of programs can influence program alternatives. If an agency insists on regulating programs by handicapping conditions, for example, it is very difficult to consider developmentally based programs as alternatives. If assistance cannot be provided, those programs requiring the least assistance are the only alternatives. Resources, of course, are an obvious consideration. How much a program alternative will cost will probably remain a prime influence on the process of selecting a program from alternatives for some time.

Sub-questions (b) and (c) draw attention to the problems of incompatibility among the three functions. This potential incompatibility can influence the selection of a program. Consider the following example: your agency tells someone, "We're here to deliver assistance in these certain areas so you can upgrade your program. If you don't upgrade your program, you cannot keep your license." People are likely to listen, but whether they act on the advice after you leave is another question. The functions of providing assistance and monitoring can sometimes be and may always be very incompatible .

4. What are the agencies currently involved in services to young, handicapped children in your state?

    a. What is the history of interagency cooperation within your state and how will this history influence program alternatives?

Interagency relationships are not easily changed. Good people with good intentions do not seem to be enough to alter the existing relationships among agencies. Thus, any alternative which involves other agencies must be considered in terms of existing relationships. If the program alternative does not require a change in the existing agency relationships, then implementation of the program will probably go smoothly. However, if a change is required, implementation will be a problem until a change in relationship has occurred.

For example, if a program alternative requires one agency to do screening and diagnosis and another agency to provide the classroom program, the program alternative will be most difficult to implement if there is not a history of information sharing between the two agencies.

5. What expectations do public schools, health and social services, private schools, day care centers, federal agencies, advocate groups, and other organizations or agencies have for the state special education agency in the area of early education for the handicapped?

    a. What impact will the above expectations have on program alternatives?

It is important to know what various professional groups, agencies, and individuals expect of the state education agency in order to calculate the consequences of their expectations on a program. For example, if day care centers expect that you are going to leave them alone or provide them with money but they do not expect you to regulate their operation, there may be severe consequences for any set of program alternatives that are developed with these expectations in mind. If local education agencies have not traditionally provided services for a particular client group and a program alternative is selected which requires the local education agency to deliver services to this set client, it could cause considerable difficulty.

The point, of course, is not that a program alternative should be eliminated because it does not conform to existing expectations. Rather, the point is that if a program alternative requires a change in expectations you must be able to change the expectations. How much the expectations can be changed will determine how successfully a program can be implemented.

6. What are the resource requirements for your alternatives? Some considerations would be: (a) state personnel training, (b) retraining of teachers, (c) how many new teachers with what kind of training, (d) curriculum materials, and (e) facilities.

Money is the first resource requirement that is usually mentioned when program alternatives are considered. The availability of financial resources is a major influence on selecting a program. When an alternative is to be implemented, it is necessary to ascertain what it is going to cost and where the funds are going to come from to meet the cost.

There are resource requirements other than money that can influence program alternatives. Any program requires the existence of a host of resources, trained personnel, facilities and materials, for example. Often, there is a tendency to assume that such resources do exist and only after a program experiences great difficulty is it clearly recognized that the needed resources were not available. If crucial resources cannot be obtained, then the influence of their absence can be extreme. This does not mean that a program should be eliminated from consideration because resources are not in place. Rather, it means that provisions should be made for the resources before a selected program alternative is implemented.

7. Is there agreement within your agency concerning the major role and function of the state special education agency in the early education of the handicapped? If the answer is no, what are the consequences and what strategies are planned to deal with the consequences?

Previously in this chapter there was a discussion of the influence of expectations and relationships among organizations on programs. Although interagency agreements and disagreements usually get far more attention than the issue of intraagency agreements, the latter can have as much influence on a program as the interagency agreements or disagreements. For example, it would be difficult to try to start a statewide early education program without the endorsement and support of the chief state school officer.

When different branches or departments of an agency are responsible for different functions within a single program, then the consequence or influence is not very different from interagency relationships. In essence, the points made in the discussion about interagency relationship and influence apply to the relationships and influences between branches within an agency.

In summary, the definition of "program" given at the beginning of this chapter can be used to analyze what part of a program will be influenced. There remains the necessity to conceptualize where the source of the influence is and the nature of that influence. The seven questions presented in this chapter were presented as examples of sources and types of influence. Furthermore, within each state, the way any source might influence an alternative must be determined.

CHAPTER 6

The Program in Washington State

Wayne Spence

To understand the program in Washington, I think first you have to understand a little bit about our state. In Washington, we have had mandatory law for the education of handicapped children since 1973. The law does not include preschool-aged children. If a local school district opts to develop a program for preschool children, however, and if our office approves that program, then the children do come under mandatory funding.

We have developed a definition for handicapped children that is more functionally than categorically oriented, both because of legislative requirements and because we need information before serving a child. While it is difficult to define a child's handicap in terms of function, we feel that such definitions are essential. Without knowledge of a child's functional level, how can resources realistically be provided to correct deficits in performance?

The Decision Process

We have developed a system in which parents must "sign-off" twice in order for their child to get into a program. First, after the pre-assessment information has been gathered, it is presented to the parent. If further evaluation is indicated, the parent is told, "With all this information, it looks like your child needs an assessment." The parents can say yes or no to an assessment. If they say no, the child will drop out of special education involvement. We do have child protection laws that cover all children to make sure that parents don't make unfortunate decisions.

After we define the child functionally, we look at him summatively and formatively, and we develop a list of the options that are available to him.

With an assessment team, we can develop long-term goals for the child. Finally, we present an option to the parent, along with the goals and a list of short term objectives. At this point, the parents enter into a contract of sorts with the local school district to put the child into the determined program.

The program must involve parents. One of the things we're trying to point out to parents is that more and more the decision making process is ending up in courts rather than with parents and educators where it belongs. With the sign-off procedure, we are trying to communicate with parents at a personal level, rather than at a legal level.

The Preschool Program

Prior to 1973 we served no handicapped children at the preschool level. In our state program this year we have 1,423 special education teachers in the classrooms, and we have 429 resource room teachers. We define a resource room teacher in our state as a teacher who has no less than twenty-six children for no more than two hours per day. We have twenty-eight agency teachers. In preschool we have only forty-two teachers.

We are trying to offer parents real educational options for their children. For example, it used to be that parents who lived in Wenatchee were told: (1) you can send your children to Seattle, or (2) you can send them to institutions. At the state level we are saying that such an offer is not an option. An option is something that allows a person to go one of several ways without feeling guilty about the choice. A situation which requires removing the child from the home is thus not an option. To improve the parents' choices, we added a contractual arrangement to our system which allowed us to enter contracts with private and parochial agencies. These contracts made it possible for children to enter programs in their own areas. We probably have seventy-five classrooms under this type of contractual arrangement in the area of preschool education.

In 1974-75, we had 740,000 children in the total school population. We had 30,000 children with special needs in the classroom. This figure does not include the children who are getting itinerant services, speech and hearing services, psychological services, and so on. In 1971, 21,000 children were in the classroom. During our next biannual budget period, the number of children with handicapping conditions will jump to approximately 35,000.

The Rural Area

We have two kinds of populations. The urban-suburban areas and the rural areas. Twenty-two percent of our children reside in rural settings. Not only have we tried to develop the classroom model for preschool early childhood education in these areas, we've also gone to the home instruction model which involves parent intervention that can be tied into a semi-structured classroom. The child may come to the class for an hour a day, usually for occupational therapy or physical therapy services. We define such service as one of the child's needs. We've augmented the home instruction model with educational service districts (which are twelve in number). These districts are service units which are charged, not with teaching children, but with assisting people who do teach children. We have educational specialists in the twelve districts. These specialists travel around to identify children in need of services or, sometimes, to identify those children who are receiving inadequate services. The specialists help the teachers develop educational programs for the children. We have found that the specialists spend a lot of their time developing preschool programs for a very small number of children. For example, we had a three-year-old deaf-blind child who lived way up in the mountains. The parents did not want to move, but they did want to keep the child at home. We talked with Dr. Norris Haring of the Experimental Education Unit (EEU) at the University of Washington about how to run an effective program for that child while allowing her to stay at home. Dr. Haring, the director of the EEU, suggested, "Why don't you bring the teacher and the aide who will be working with the child to the EEU for several weeks of training. You can let them look at some of the behaviors they may see in the child, teach them about continuous measurement, and then send them back over the mountains. Every Thursday morning at 9:00 A.M. you can call them to see what happened in the past week's program." On both ends of the line, teachers kept data. Every Thursday at 9:00 A.M., the child's program for the next week was established. There were about ten people on the University of Washington side of the line who were helping to program for that child. At the end of the program, the child was near grade level. Such is the type of alternative program we must provide, and it can only work with cooperation from people in and out of education throughout the state.

Other Programs

SEMAT. The other program that we use as a backup or services system is the SEMAT centers. SEMAT stands for Special Education, Materials, and

Training centers. In these centers, we train teachers in the use of materials and equipment, in programming for kids, etc. The centers are spread around the state, but they mainly provide services for children outside the first (or urban) districts. The SEMAT centers can be very useful to both parents and teachers involved in preschool programs in the rural areas. They provide not only training services but free materials and equipment. SEMAT has been an excellent addition to our state effort, and it has brought statewide recognition. We plan to continue SEMAT even after federal funding is discontinued.

Health and Social Services. We have had some interchange with the Department of Social and Health Services. Efforts to establish a viable liaison between the state education agency and Social and Health Services has taken much time. Ms. Epton was a lady senator who had great concern for handicapped children. She developed a law to insure that very young children who weren't in the general educational program because they weren't allowed would be served educationally through centers. These centers were set up fifteen years ago, and they are still operating. The problem that Social and Health Services is concerned with right now is legislative. The department would like to phase out all of the Epton programs and transfer their kids into the educational program under our direction. We would be happy to accept the children, but first we must get the law changed so that these children fall under mandatory legislation. We haven't accomplished that yet, but we're working on it.

Advisory Councils. We do not have an advisory council for the preschool area. We have only one advisory council for all of special education. We have found it advantageous for our one council to split up into task forces (e.g., early childhood) as we have needs in particular areas.

Training. We have to start placing some of our money into the regular education program at the preschool and kindergarten level to help prepare teachers to deal with the handicapped children that they are going to inherit, especially in the rural and remote areas. We plan to put the dollars available, both from the state and the federal governments, into some retraining programs for regular classroom teachers who are dealing with handicapped children at the preschool level. It's been a very stormy marriage with regular education; we're both going to have to try to soften up because our total existence is strongly tied to regular education even though we have a separate funding base.

CHAPTER 7

The Program in Virginia

Wayne B. Largent

There were two major issues involved in developing a state plan for the education of preschool handicapped children in Virginia: categorical legislation and the child's age. The categorical legislation provided education for children with the following conditions: mental retardation, emotional disturbance, physical handicaps (other categories), and any other such condition as may be determined by the State Board of Education. Using the legislative option available to state boards of education, we created the following developmental definition for "handicapped": "A handicapped child is one who deviates significantly from established milestones or norms in motor, adaptive and social, sensory, and/or language development."

The second issue involved in developing the state plan was age. The legislation declared that persons two to twenty-one, or any other such age as may be determined by the state board, were to be served. After the legislation was enacted, the state board was asked to exercise its option by lowering the age range to birth. Because state officials were uneasy about mandating services for children aged zero to two before they had a chance to provide service to children in the three- to five- age range, the following option was included in the state plan:

> This plan is designed to fulfill the mandatory requirement for provision of services to handicapped children from two to five years of age. The program with state support is available on a permissive basis to children below age two if the school division elects to provide service for the very young.

By providing services to the very young handicapped child, we hoped to document the soundness of very early intervention (below the age of two).

The Virginia Comprehensive State Plan begins with the assumption that a target population has been identified by a statewide system of Child Development Clinics. The first step in the plan is that a clinic refers a child to a superintendent who determines whether the child is a responsibility of the division by answering the question: "Is the child a *resident* of this division?" If the answer is "Yes," the referral is transferred to the individual responsible for planning the educational program, the Child Development Specialist (CDS). Each local school division should, according to the plan, employ a CDS whose function is to study each child's needs, convene placement committees, and initiate parent programs. Some of the questions which must be answered in studying each child's needs include: (1) Are programs available? (2) If not, can a program be developed? (3) Can a program be purchased? (4) Are appropriate services available through other agencies? If the answer to each question is "No," the next step is to contact the State Department of Education for technical assistance.

After the availability of services has been determined, the placement of a child into an appropriate program occurs. The Plan declares that not more than twenty working days shall pass between the time a child is referred to the superintendent and the time that a program for that child begins. "Begins" can be defined as "the time involvement with parents and family is initiated."

After a child has entered a program, the CDS must monitor his progress and make sure that the program is appropriate for his needs. By careful monitoring, the CDS helps the child move toward an easy transfer into a school-age program.

Two other major activities are covered in the implementation phase of the Virginia State Plan. One involves initiating a training program for the role of Child Development Specialist. We felt that people trained in child development were needed if the State Plan were going to work. The other activity involves the development of one delivery strategy that can be made available to all the local school divisions in the state. The strategy selected is a home-based program that involves the use of a parent or parent substitute (paraprofessional) in a one-to-one situation with the child. The use of paraprofessionals, aided by specific developmental materials that we are preparing (in some instances, by modifying those which are already available), makes it possible for preschool children in the various counties to have programs which address their individual developmental stages and learning patterns.

At this point [February 1975], we are trying to make services available statewide by September 1975. Those services will include the home-based delivery system and the Child Development Specialists. We hope the CDS's will be able to gather some data to be used in modifying the Plan and validating the materials. The revision of materials will help us implement full services, according to our legislation, by the 1976-77 school year.

CHAPTER 8

The Program in New Jersey

Tealey L. Collins

Legislation designed to provide educational services to preschool handicapped children was first introduced in the New Jersey State Legislature in 1970 as Senate Bill 441. That bill is still in the legislature's Educational Committee waiting to be enacted into law. So while the state has made a commitment to establishing programs for the preschool handicapped, it has been unable to realize the full potential of that commitment.

In 1974, the state legislature appropriated $500,000 for the development of pilot projects for preschool handicapped children. The State Department of Education (Branch of Special Education and Pupil Personnel Services) was given the responsibility of planning for the development of the projects. (The original allocation was increased to $1,000,000 in fiscal year 1975.) Fifteen projects, which were approved for funding, provided for screening, identification, and evaluation of three- and four-year-old handicapped children in a classroom setting. In addition to funding these projects, the Department of Education funded Rutgers University (Graduate School of Education) to develop and implement a statewide training program for parents of preschool handicapped children. This paper addresses the Rutgers segment of the New Jersey State Program for the Preschool Handicapped.

The Rutgers Parent Training Program is designed to train parents of preschool handicapped children to implement an individualized, prescriptive, home teaching program in an effort to ameliorate their children's handicapping conditions. One underlying assumption of the Program is that parents are the primary teachers of their children. Another assumption is that to become effective educational change agents with their children, and to make lasting changes, parents must become involved in the educational process.

The population served are those preschool children within the state who are diagnosed as handicapped according to definitions of "handicapped" in the New Jersey Education of the Handicapped statutes. The types of handicaps served in the program are: trainable mentally retarded; educable mentally retarded; specific learning disabilities; deaf-blind; deaf; hard of hearing; visually handicapped; seriously emotionally disturbed; speech impaired; other health impaired; and crippled.

The first years of program implementation were 1973-74. During that time, thirteen counties were involved in providing parent training services. During 1974-75, the pilot effort became a statewide program providing parent training in every county of the state. The number of children receiving services had increased from 250 to 500.

Goals of Parent Training

The specific goals of the Rutgers Parent Training Program are:

1. To increase the understanding of the effects of positive and negative reinforcement on learning.

2. To impart to the parent a knowledge of the developmental sequence and the ages at which developmental skills usually appear.

3. To encourage the parent to engage in verbal interaction with the handicapped child more frequently.

Training Staff and Parents

The individuals who train and work with parents are called Parent Advisors (PA's). The background of the Parent Advisors is primarily education, although a few are from the social work and psychology fields. After the Parent Advisors have been chosen, the training process begins. The procedure involves the following:

1. An orientation program is provided to introduce the staff of PA's to the overall preschool program.

2. Following orientation, the PA's undergo a training program designed to help trainees (a) master the skills which are necessary to use the parent education materials successfully and to convey the proper use

of the materials to parents; (b) learn to recognize and apply the basic behavioral principles of positive and negative reinforcement, punishment, and extinction; (c) develop the assessment skills needed to develop a profile of the child's developmental level and to teach these skills to the parents; (d) learn to write adequate behavioral prescriptions for identifying target behavior and developing baseline behaviors; and (e) to be sensitive to the parents' understanding of the materials presented.

3. Next, Parent Advisors begin to recruit their family caseloads. Upon learning of potential parent or child and parent enrollees, the Parent Advisor visits the homes for the purposes of determining program eligibility and explaining participation requirements.

4. The Parent Advisor then familiarizes himself or herself with each family and determines, through discussion with the parents, the most effective and convenient way in which to deliver the content of the parent training program.

5. Parents are now ready to receive their initial (intensive) training which will last for a few weeks and will continue throughout their participation period. The introductory training is designed (a) to define the overall concept of the program and the role of the parents; (b) to demonstrate the use of the instructional materials; (c) to teach entry skills in developmental profiling and educational prescription writing; and, (d) to introduce the basic concepts of behavior management.

6. Upon completion of the initial training period, the home visits begin and the individual parent training is transferred into the home.

The basic goals of the home visits are to support the parents in the home teaching process and to continue training activities as the parents advance. A typical home visit is conducted in the following manner.

The parent and Parent Advisor discuss the child's progress in mastering the task outlined in a previously written behavioral description. If success has been achieved, the parent works with the child in demonstrating mastery of the skill or task. From this demonstration, a new prescription is written.

If success has not been achieved, the parent and PA try to determine the cause(s): e.g., the prescription (task) was too difficult; directions were not clearly stated; the child would not cooperate; the parent did not work with the child, etc.

If a new prescription is written, the Parent Advisor demonstrates the activity to the parent and then requests that the parent try the activity with the child. The remaining time is devoted to discussing other areas of parent interest.

Additional Support

The home-based parents often lack a focal point, such as a formal preschool site. Their contact is a weekly or monthly home visit from their Parent Advisor. Many parents in the Program have stated that they feel very much alone and desire to meet other parents of preschool handicapped children. Monthly group meetings, consequently, became a part of the parent training format. The meetings not only provide an opportunity for parents to interact, but they also create a climate for developing the social and emotional support which parents seem to need.

PART THREE

PLANNING COMPREHENSIVE SERVICES

CHAPTER 9

Identifying and Planning Services for Children

David L. Lillie

To improve the life of a handicapped child, a variety of services must be available to both child and parents very early. Clearly, it is not enough to provide only educational services when the child has needs which demand the attentions of many different professionals. Unfortunately, the number of services which should be offered is often difficult to determine.

Personnel at the state education agency level should address the question of "What services should be provided?" Each agency should determine (1) what it considers to be a comprehensive set of services and (2) whether or not the state education agency should provide only educational services or whether it should assume the coordination of comprehensive services. In this chapter, the range of services that should be offered by a state is discussed, and the particular services that should be offered in various areas are outlined.

The range of services that should be available for young children should include: casefinding, screening, diagnostic services, education, therapy, health and nutrition, social services, counseling, and services for families. This range of services may not be part of each child's individual program, but each service should be available if needed. (For more information on these services, see Part IV.)

Educational Services, as defined by Public Law 94-142 (see Appendix A), should be based on an individual educational plan. Educational services need to address not only the weaknesses but the strengths of the child in all areas of development. It is not uncommon for programs for young handicapped children to be deficit-oriented, i.e., to disregard areas of development not affected by the deficit.

The importance of providing *services to families* of young handicapped children is no longer debatable. It is clear that parents play a vital role and are the most important adults in a young child's life. To develop a program that does not include services for parents will have little long-term impact on the child. Services for families might include training parents to teach their child, providing a family with counseling, helping the parents accept their child's handicaps, developing a link between home and school, and referral to other community agencies. Providers of services to families might be mental health agencies, social service agencies, the medical community, and private practitioners such as psychologists.

Physical, occupational, and speech therapy are vital during the early years if a child requires therapy to profit from other services, particularly education. Coordination between the educational staff, the parent and clinicians can enhance the child's progress from one therapy session to the other and insure that skills gained through therapy become generalizable.

Health, medical, and nutritional services need to be within the range of services provided to a child. The involvement of health fields begins with screening and diagnosis. Health input often adds a new perspective to the diagnosis and treatment of a child's handicapping condition. Corrective surgery for a young physically handicapped child can prevent emotional and secondary handicaps. Medication can greatly enhance the ability of the child with seizures to profit from an educational program. Because services can often be very expensive for families, efforts need to be made to help families obtain financial aid, if needed, as well as to locate the appropriate professionals.

The first step in providing comprehensive services is locating existing services. This chapter presents a conceptual matrix which can be used for that purpose. Each state using the matrix may have to redefine the categories within some of the major dimensions to fit their state laws and definitions.

The matrix has three major dimensions: the degree of severity of the handicapping condition, the age of the child, and the type of service. (See the last three pages of the chapter for a breakdown of the matrix into each of these dimensions.) The first dimension allows the user to consider the need for services in his or her state in relation to the severity of the handicapping condition. What constitutes mild, moderate, or severe handicaps? If we go to the textbooks, we find that a child who has a mild problem is one who, as he grows older, becomes independent from assistance and

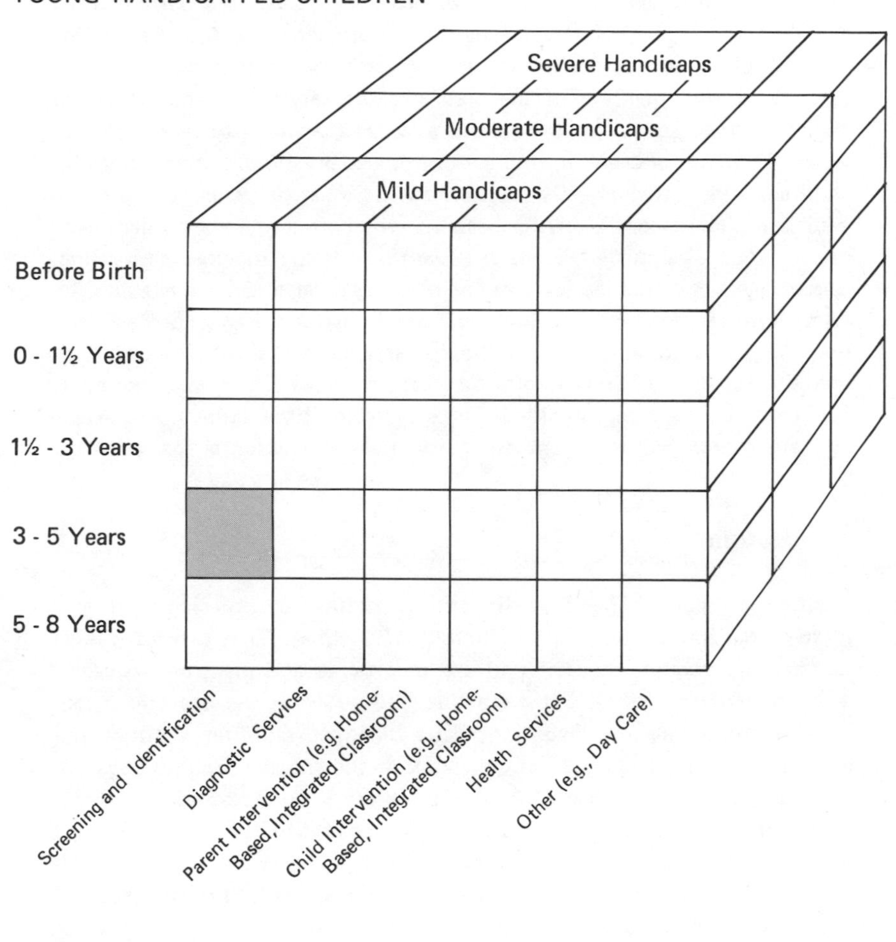
COMPREHENSIVE SERVICES FOR
YOUNG HANDICAPPED CHILDREN
Severe Handicaps
Moderate Handicaps
Mild Handicaps
Before Birth
0 - 1½ Years
1½ - 3 Years
3 - 5 Years
5 - 8 Years
Screening and Identification
Diagnostic Services
Parent Intervention (e.g. Home-Based, Integrated Classroom)
Child Intervention (e.g., Home-Based, Integrated Classroom)
Health Services
Other (e.g., Day Care)

does not need continuing help as an adult. A child with a moderate handicap is more dependent on assistance, but some independence can be established. The severely handicapped child will probably need some kind of assistance throughout his life, depending on the community and the kinds of assistance that are being offered.

Another dimension of the matrix is age. The categories are: before birth, birth to one-and-a-half years, one-and-a-half to three years, three to five years, and five years to eight years. These age groupings have been used because there are similar developmental activities in which most children in each of the given age groups are involved. For example, children of ages five through eight may be involved in academic activities, while three- through five-year-olds are usually in pre-academic activities. These age groupings reflect the trends in the delivery of preschool services.

The third dimension of the matrix is the service component which allows the user to specify the various services that need to be or are provided. The first element in intervention is usually *Finding and Screening* children. After screening, *Diagnostic Services* must be available to provide a differential diagnosis on the basis of which treatment and placement decisions can be made. *Parent Intervention,* which includes counseling, educational, and training services for parents, must also be available. The *Child Intervention Services* include home-based programs, center-based programs, and combinations of these. Certainly for those working with young preschool children, *Health Services* are more and more prominent. Services that are being provided primarily from *Other Educational Agencies* are extremely important to consider in any comprehensive effort.

Application

Taking into account the three dimensions outlined and placing them in a matrix, we end up with approximately 120 cubes. That creates a huge number of program needs if you are to provide and identify services in every one of the cubes. Let's examine one cube on the chart in detail.

Screening three- to five-year-old handicapped children is not an uncommon area of service. When you look at the shaded cube on page 63, you should ask a number of questions. What is your state doing in this area? What agency has administrative responsibility for these children? Are there any laws which assign responsibility? Are there any interpretations of the laws which indicate who has the responsibility? Are there no laws but activities going on in that area which indicate that an agency has assumed the responsibility by default? What implications would such a default have for your own program? If you find that this cube is the responsibility of the mental health agency, for example, what does this finding mean for the education agency? It may mean that screening activities will have to be coordinated with planning for services at some time in the future. Another question to consider is: Who is actually doing the screening——where, when, and how?

As you can see, for each cube you must ask a series of questions: (1) What agency has the responsibility? (2) What kinds of professionals, paraprofessionals, or volunteers are actually doing the work? (3) Where (statewide, regionally, locally) is it happening? (5) When (immediately? over a twelve-month period? etc.) will the activities take place?

The matrix should be considered carefully before it is used for planning and identifying services in a state. Perhaps the following question needs to be asked: Does this matrix actually incorporate all possible services? It may be necessary to identify more dimensions and more questions for each cube. In other words, the matrix is a tool to assist you in your planning. It should be adapted to the specific planning needs and relationships of the education agency in your state.

Finally, consider using the matrix in coordinating activities among agencies in the state. The matrix is an excellent tool for mapping out responsibilities and indicating gaps in services.

When comparing what exists with what should exist, planners may find interesting trends such as sparse services in one region, abundant services in another, adequate services for the severe and profoundly handicapped but nothing for the mildly handicapped, and duplication of services. Planning for adequate services and filling existing gaps may require coordinated interagency planning and implementation, passage of new legislation, reallocation of resources, or enforcement of existing legislation.

The provision of comprehensive services to children is difficult because professionals and agencies end up competing for children, protecting their domain, and not being given the authority, responsibility or resources to provide the services. It is only after barriers are removed and professionals see interagency services to young handicapped children as a common goal that we will begin to develop the comprehensive range of services that will make a long term difference in the life of the young handicapped child.

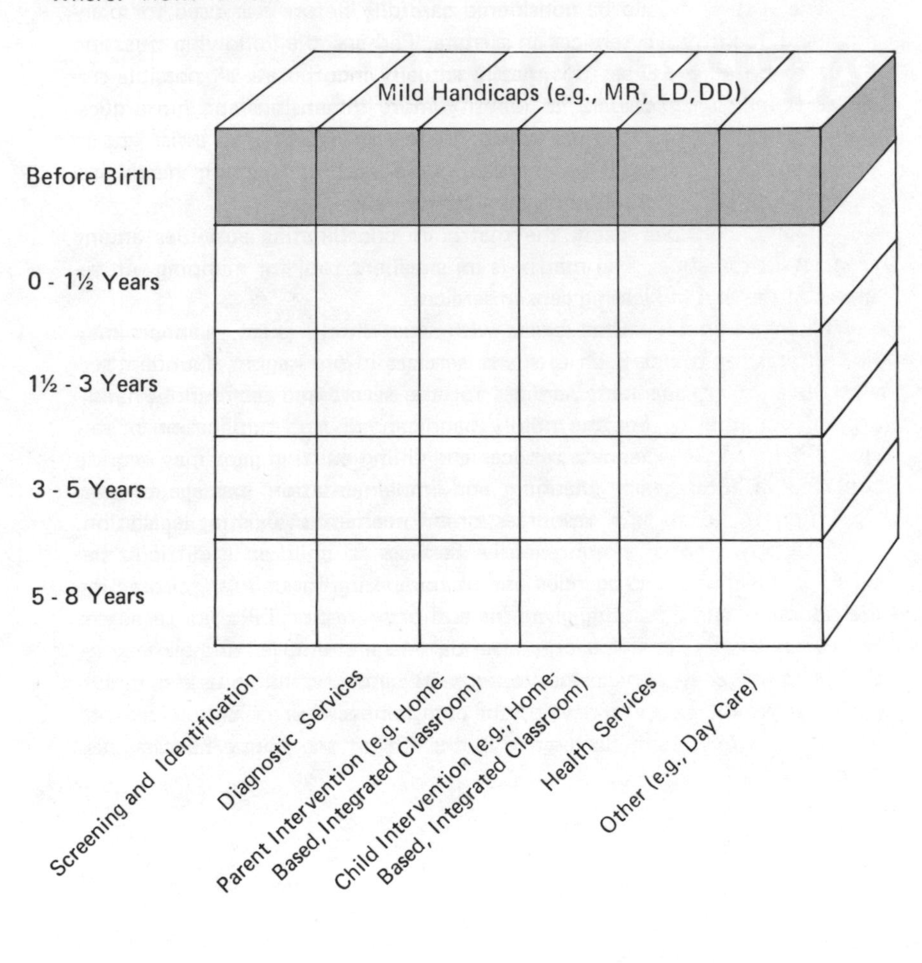
For each cube, answer:
Who administers?
Who executes?
Where? How? When?
Mild Handicaps (e.g., MR, LD, DD)
Before Birth
0 - 1½ Years
1½ - 3 Years
3 - 5 Years
5 - 8 Years
Screening and Identification
Diagnostic Services
Parent Intervention (e.g. Home-Based, Integrated Classroom)
Child Intervention (e.g. Home-Based, Integrated Classroom)
Health Services
Other (e.g., Day Care)

For each cube, answer:
Who administers?
Who executes?
Where? How? When?

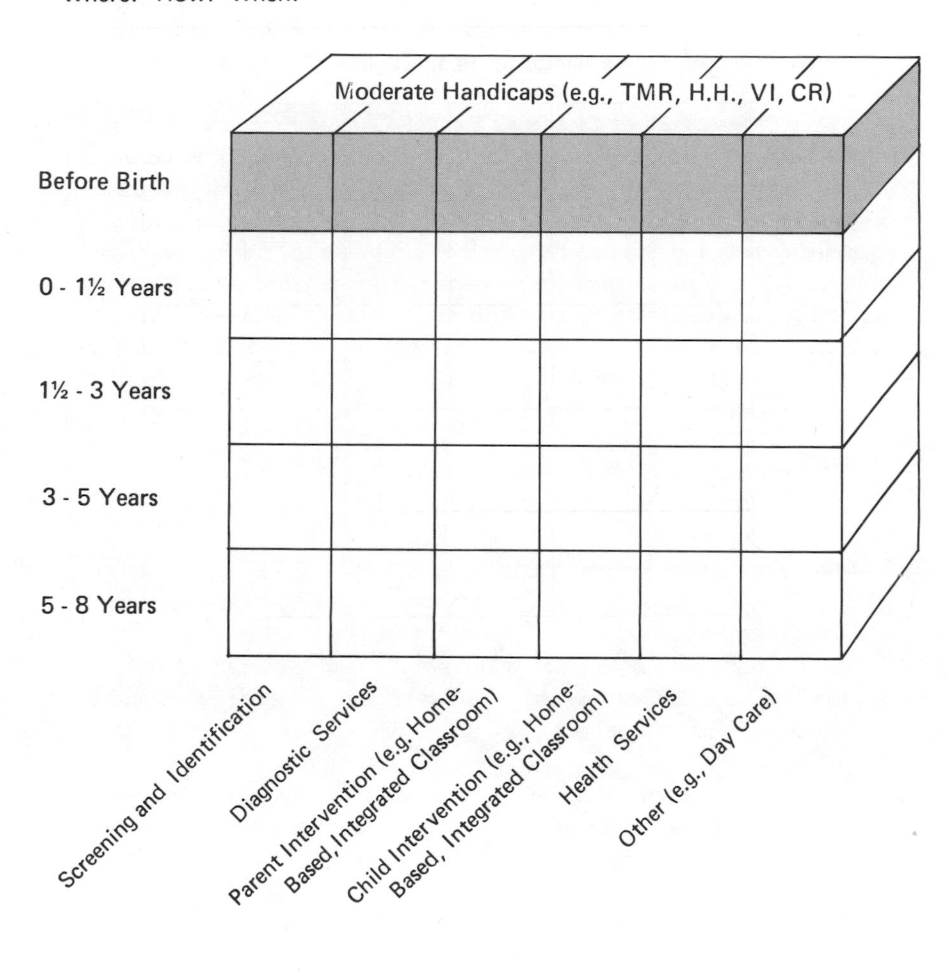

For each cube, answer:
Who administers?
Who executes?
Where? How? When?

Severe Handicaps (e.g., CP, MR, Of., Bl., Multi-H.)

Before Birth

0 - 1½ Years

1½ - 3 Years

3 - 5 Years

5 - 8 Years

Screening and Identification

Diagnostic Services

Parent Intervention (e.g. Home-Based, Integrated Classroom)

Child Intervention (e.g., Home-Based, Integrated Classroom)

Health Services

Other (e.g., Day Care)

CHAPTER 10

Using a Matrix Approach in Identifying Services

Anne L. Connolly and Ruth Ann Rasbold

In the State of Massachusetts, we attempted to utilize the matrix presented in the preceding chapter.

As a point of information and reference, it should be noted that Chapter 776 of the Acts of 1972 requires that seven state agencies work cooperatively in promulgating regulations for children with special needs. The Intersecretariat Meeting, which is attended by the Secretaries of Human Services (public health, mental health, youth services, welfare, and various related agencies) and Education, is designed to help the agencies involved decide "who is responsible for what" and "who pays for what." This is especially important because Chapter 766 of the Acts of 1972, (Public Law 93-230) the Comprehensive Special Education Law, mandates that local education agencies are responsible for the education of children from three to twenty-one. Although the law mandates cooperation among seven state agencies, the monies actually have remained in the same agencies in which they have always been. This is one of the biggest problems faced by the local education agencies. They feel very strongly that if they are responsible for all screening and identification, evaluation, and program planning, some of the monies that are presently sitting in mental health, public health, and in youth services should be shared.

Information Search

One of the problems in finding the information in the matrix was not only that some agencies did not know what other agencies were doing but, people didn't even know what the people sitting next to them were doing; they didn't even know what services their own agency provided. Thus, we often ended up calling several people within the same agency to obtain the necessary information.

We asked these people, "What services do you provide? Are you providing these services because it's mandated or are you assuming that responsibility? What is the extent of your service; do you just deal with the parents; do you just deal with the children; do you combine the two; do you identify and screen, or do you just take the kids after they have been diagnosed? What ages do you serve?"

The degree of handicaps presented in the matrix (mild, moderate, and severe) had to be redefined. Instead of saying "mild handicaps," we used the phrase "high risk." In place of "moderately handicapped," we used the term "developmentally handicapped." For "severely handicapped," we used the terms "multiply handicapped" and "physically disabled" (blind, deaf, etc.).

Results

The results of collecting the information for the matrix were interesting. For example, in the preschool services component, we found that for the ages of birth through two, the Bureau of Developmental Disabilities had funded several programs. The Department of Mental Health had also started and approved a grant for that age group. At the age of two, the Department of Mental Health started picking up children that were formally called "mentally retarded." They expanded their services with the term "developmentally delayed," which includes anybody physically or mentally retarded, whether they have physical delays, mental delays, and/or emotional delays.

When the children reach the age of three, the local education agencies become responsible for them. We found that all state agencies have something going on for ages three up. We're in the process of trying to get all *educational* services under the Department of Education. It's a slow process; other agencies do not want to give up their responsibility, and the local education agencies are somewhat reluctant to take the responsibility for three-year-old children.

When children are five (kindergarten age) and above, local education agencies are more willing to provide services because they have programs already set up. They have some idea of the kind of screening instruments to use, and they have programs to place the children and are able to modify their present programs.

Another interesting point is that some program components are being implemented without a legislative mandate, simply because an agency determined that there was a need for a particular service. For instance, the Department of Public Health has assumed the responsibility of providing some prenatal education care for mothers. They did so because they knew it was needed, not because anybody asked them to do it. We also found that most services for children below the age of two were the result of pressure groups and not the result of legislation.

Conclusion

Generally, after we reached the people we needed to reach and got the information on the right form, we had a good visual layout of what was going on. We knew areas in which nothing is being done, while we knew that adequate services were provided in other areas. The greatest need is for coordination not only between, but within, agencies. Many times, one agency doesn't even realize that another agency is having the same program. Somebody needs to know what everybody is doing in order to avoid duplication of services and encourage maximum utilization of resources.

PART FOUR

IDENTIFICATION SERVICES

CHAPTER 11

Identification of Young Children with Handicaps: An Overview

Lee Cross

Because of the thrust of Public Law 93-380, many states are involved in activities to identify children with handicaps. It has become increasingly apparent that there is confusion about the terminology, definitions, and procedures that are being used in the identification efforts. Casefinding, screening, and diagnosis are the three procedures that state education agencies are currently involved in implementing. Assessment, which closely follows diagnosis in an identification treatment program, will also be discussed here because of its central importance in any educational treatment program. It is hoped that this overview will provide clarification and stimulate sound procedures for the identification of young handicapped children.

An Overview of Identification Procedures

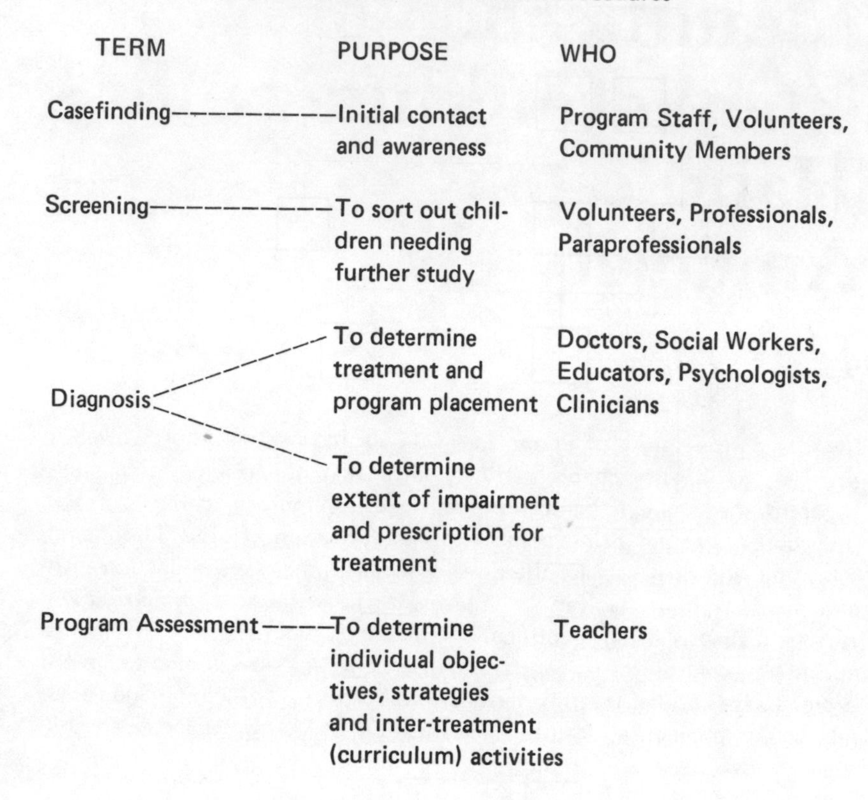

TERM	PURPOSE	WHO
Casefinding	Initial contact and awareness	Program Staff, Volunteers, Community Members
Screening	To sort out children needing further study	Volunteers, Professionals, Paraprofessionals
Diagnosis	To determine treatment and program placement	Doctors, Social Workers, Educators, Psychologists, Clinicians
	To determine extent of impairment and prescription for treatment	
Program Assessment	To determine individual objectives, strategies and inter-treatment (curriculum) activities	Teachers

Casefinding. Casefinding is a systematic process for locating children with handicaps or potential handicaps who will profit from early intervention services. Depending on the program's goals and objectives, casefinding may be part of those procedures involved in locating children for screening or diagnostic activities. The casefinding process includes defining the target population, increasing the public's awareness of services, encouraging referrals, and canvassing the community for children.

The casefinding procedures selected by a program depend on the nature of the target population. For example, a project serving children from birth through two years of age within a fifty mile radius might only need to contact all pediatricians and newborn care units in hospitals within fifty miles. Whereas, a project whose target is three- through five-year-old children with mild mental handicaps will undoubtedly have to advertise its services, solicit referrals from social service and health agencies, and canvass neighborhoods.

One of the initial steps in casefinding is developing the public's awareness through education of the importance of early identification. Awareness strategies include brochures, newspaper articles, speaking engagements, radio and television spots, posters, and contacting agencies. Public awareness activities must take place irrespective of the severity of the target group's handicapping condition. It is usually not beneficial to rely solely on awareness activities to find children because of the impersonal nature of this approach.

Another strategy for locating children with handicaps is to develop contacts with agencies serving both handicapped and non-handicapped preschool children. Agencies should be contacted both as a part of your awareness program and as a referral source. Whenever possible, efforts should be made to coordinate, not duplicate, services. This procedure is particularly effective in locating children with severe handicaps; it is not as effective in locating children with moderate and mild impairments who may not be known to other agencies.

Contact with agencies and services might be made personally or by letter. An exact description of the population to be served, as well as the range of services to be provided, should be furnished to each agency.

Examples of agencies which should be contacted are: public schools; health, welfare, and social services; community day care, nursery, and preschool programs; agencies serving handicapped children (such as Easter Seals, United Cerebral Palsy, Crippled Children, Association for Retarded Children, mental health facilities, speech and language clinics, and diagnostic clinics). Private practitioners such as therapists, pediatricians, psychologists, and psychiatrists should also be informed of the availability of program services.

One of the most effective casefinding procedures is a door-to-door census that is designed to locate and register all children within a specified age range in a community. This is particularly effective for identifying children with moderate and/or mild impairments or when the objective is to screen all preschool children.

Another procedure that may be used in canvassing the community is sending forms home with school-age children and children in day care, nursery school, and Head Start which request parents to fill out information on the preschool children in their families. Also, a preschool "round-up" requesting parents to register their child at a designated location might be held. These two methods, while less costly and time consuming, are not as effective as a door to door campaign in that they rely on parents being literate and utilizing local media.

Screening. Screening is the measurement activity which identifies in the general population those children that appear to be in need of special services in order to develop to their maximum potential. The intent of screening is to review a large number of children for a particular handicap (or deviance in development) in a fast and efficient way. For example, in Smith County there are 1,000 children between ages three and five. If the goal of the program is to identify and provide services to all county children with delays in two or more developmental areas, the most efficient and economical first step in the identification process would be to screen all three- to five-year-old children in the county to find those with possible developmental delays. On the other hand, if the goal is to identify and provide services to all three- to five-year-old cerebral palsied children, then county-wide screening would probably not be the most appropriate procedure to use because it would be time consuming and expensive. In most cases, it is not necessary to screen for severe handicaps because this population can be identified during casefinding.

Results of screening should provide staff with enough information about a child to decide (1) if he is a candidate for thorough diagnostic study or (2) if at the present time he has a good prognosis for success without receiving special services.

Screening is a source of valuable information about the development of children, but it has its limitations in that it can only indicate the possible presence of an impairment. Therefore, children should *not* be labelled on the basis of screening, and intervention should not be determined or planned without diagnostic study.

In selecting a screening instrument, you need to establish criteria for selecting an instrument which will provide the greatest amount of desirable data. Some considerations are:

1. What problem, impairment, or handicap is being screened?

   In selecting an instrument, you need to consider the nature of the problem. Is it health, physical, language, motor, developmental? Only instruments which screen those problems which can be treated by the program or referred to another agency in the community should be selected.

2. Is the selected procedure reliable, valid, and standardized?

   Since the purpose of screening is to sort out from the general population those children who need further study, a screening instrument needs to be selected which is reliable, valid, and standardized.

3. Who will administer the screening instrument?

   It is important to determine if screening will be administered by trained professionals (i.e., psychologists, language therapists) or paraprofessionals, trained volunteers, or parents. This decision will be influenced largely by economic considerations and by the time constraints of the professional staff.

4. How much time per child will the instrument take to administer?

   If a large number of children are to be screened, then procedures should be relatively short (probably no longer than forty-five minutes to an hour).

5. Can the instrument be easily administered?

   If trained paraprofessionals, volunteers, and/or parents will administer the instrument, then ease of administration is an important factor.

Frequently, parent questionnaires are coupled with screening instruments to aid in the identification process. Parents are extremely good observers of their own children, and they have little difficulty in sharing their observations when the questions directed to them deal with the child's usual daily activities. On the other hand, questions which deal with activities which are unusual or infrequent bring unreliable responses.

Screening should take place only if appropriate diagnostic and program services are available. If such services are unavailable, the costs expended in screening activities, as well as the unnecessary anxiety created in the parents of children identified as being in need of further examination, are unjustifiable.

Parents should be informed of the purpose and of the procedures to be used in the screening program. They should also be told the results. In cases where a child fails screening, the parent should be made aware that the child needs further diagnosis before any conclusive decisions can be made about his suspected condition.

Diagnosis. Diagnostic procedures involve looking at a child and his environment in depth:

1. to determine whether a handicapping condition (or conditions) exists,

2. to clarify the causes of the identified problem (i.e., is the child non-verbal due to a hearing impairment, mental retardation, an information-process problem, or lack of verbal stimulation),

3. to develop a treatment plan,

4. to ascertain the most appropriate service that the program can render the child.

Diagnosis is more specific than screening and ideally should involve a multi-disciplinary team of trained professionals. The composition of this multi-disciplinary team varies according to the nature of the child's disability. In determining the composition of the team, one must initially decide the type of data needed to determine the appropriate program service and treatment for the child. Data should be obtained from as many disciplines as possible in order to obtain as broad a picture as possible of the child's performance. Individuals who might be involved in the diagnosis are: a physician, a psychologist, a social worker, an educational diagnostician, a neurologist, a psychiatrist, a physical therapist, and a language therapist.

It is important that the multi-disciplinary team utilize information, such as screening results, that is already available. The screening results should give direction in prescribing further evaluations. For example, if a child passes the hearing and vision screening, it would be a waste of time to do a more in-depth evaluation in these areas. However, if a child, on the basis of screening results, shows a delay in the language area, it would be advantageous to have a speech and language clinician do a more in-depth examination. Diagnostic procedures are costly and time consuming. Therefore, it is important to keep in mind that personnel should not be involved in data collection unless their expertise and information is genuinely warranted, i.e., unless it will improve the decision making capabilities of the multi-disciplinary team.

Procedures within the diagnostic phase include the administration of standardized instruments, systematic observation, obtaining social and case histories, and formal interviews.

After the appropriate data has been obtained and analyzed, the multidisciplinary team, along with the parent(s), should synthesize and interpret the combined results as a group in order to reach agreement on the findings. A treatment plan should be developed along with recommendations for educational programming.

Once the treatment plan has been determined, appropriate services should be considered and options analyzed. It will often be necessary for supportive services as well as the educational service to be identified. It is helpful for parents if the multi-disciplinary team can identify and facilitate the referral.

Assessment. The information obtained from the results of the diagnostic activities should have strong implications for developing an individualized program for each child. This information should not be discarded once the child is placed in an appropriate program. Results should be interpreted to staff and parents with emphasis on implications for the planning of daily activities for the child.

Assessment occurs following diagnosis and placement. It involves those ongoing procedures during which the teacher and/or parent determines individual goals and objectives in specific areas of development in order to plan an individual program for the child.

The outcome of the assessment process should be a profile of the Individual to enable those working with the child to identify strengths as well as weaknesses. Assessment provides the teacher with a vehicle for planning a series of specific curriculum experiences that are based on specific goals and objectives related to the information derived from assessment.

Standardized or norm referencedtests customarily are not used by the teacher in assessing a child for the planning of an education program, although they may provide helpful information. The two most common procedures used by teachers in assessing children are criterion referenced measurements and informal assessment techniques.

Criterion referenced measures are constructed to yield data that are interpretable in terms of a specific standard of performance. Criterion referenced measures are behavioral and are stated in outcome objectives; thus results can be simply translated into appropriate curriculum objectives for each child. Individual items in a criterion referenced measure are often based on standardized items in a number of developmental scales.

Examples of informal assessment procedures include anecdotal records, observational reports, daily logs, and videotapes. These techniques are useful in understanding how the child relates to his environment, interrelates with others, and feels about himself. They are useful in noting interests, use of language, and patterns of adjustment. For informal techniques to be of value, they must be recorded systematically and precisely over a period of time so the recorder can determine the pattern and frequency of behavior.

CHAPTER 12

Considerations for Screening

William K. Frankenburg

Originally, the purpose of screening was to identify individuals who had infectious diseases (e.g., tuberculosis and syphilis) which could be transmitted to other members of the population. After World War II, when infectious diseases in developed countries came to be better controlled, screening began to be used in efforts to prevent chronic health problems. By identifying such problems early, treatment could be begun earlier and, possibly, long-term handicapping conditions could be prevented.

As screening has grown in use, several problems have developed. Many of the problems center on the fact that doctors and educators are being asked—without regard to cost or effectiveness—to screen for all kinds of conditions.

In this chapter, a script which was prepared for medical students and physicians (but which will prove equally useful for educators) is presented. It contains a brief history of screening, a set of principles which will be found useful in deciding *what* to screen for and how to screen for it, and some examples of screening situations. After the script, there is a discussion section in which the concepts involved in educational screening are discussed.

History

During the past few decades, dramatic changes have occurred in the practice of pediatrics. Among these changes is the tremendous expansion in the delivery of preventive health care to children. Screening is a major concern in this effort. Many professional organizations have recently endorsed the concept of screening, and they're recommending that their members incorporate screening into their practices. The general public is also demanding screening as part of preventive health services. This is evidenced in the 1967 amendment to the Social Security Act requiring the early and periodic screening, diagnosis and treatment (EPSDT) of all children on Medicaid. This group includes approximately twelve million individuals between birth and twenty-one years of age.

Why this emphasis on screening? Chronic conditions (e.g., vision and hearing problems) often have long silent periods before symptoms become obvious. Screening can often uncover these conditions in the early stage so that treatment can be given before serious damage results. With the increasing awareness of the value of screening, information regarding screening and screening procedures is accumulating faster than the health care provider can sort it out. Unfortunately, much of this information is contradictory.

Lists of conditions recommended for screening differ among various authorities. To complicate matters further, the effectiveness of screening varies with the community and population served, so that recommendations do not automatically apply to each situation. There are many unanswered questions about the etiology of chronic conditions, but until further research provides definite answers, the health care provider must make difficult decisions about screening. He must determine what conditions to screen for, what procedures to use, who will do the screening, when it should be done, and what it will cost in terms of time, effort, and money. This requires an approach which is quite different than that used in crisis care where the patient with symptoms presents himself.

Screening decisions about chronic conditions involve issues and principles that are much more abstract and subjective than those involved in acute illness. Administrative, ethical, social, and even political factors must often be considered. These factors must be weighed carefully to determine how a screening effort can be most beneficial and practical in the health care provider's particular situation.

Twelve screening criteria will be presented in this chapter. These criteria focus on the two major problems that must be faced in setting up a screening program. The first is the evaluation of and selection of conditions which should be screened for. The second is the evaluation of the screening procedures to be used. All of these criteria are fairly obvious once presented; yet they are easily overlooked if not pointed out. They represent the major issues around which screening decisions should be made and further research should center.

Definition

Screening is an efficient way of sorting out from an apparently well population those individuals who risk having the condition being screened for and are therefore in need of additional evaluation. Screening procedures are not diagnostic tools, and they may not be used as a substitute for periodic health examinations. Rather, screening is a practical first step leading to diagnosis and treatment. It should be viewed as a continuous process, beginning at preconception and being repeated during the course of the individual's life. With this definition of screening in mind, let's return to the criteria for making screening decisions.

Criteria for Selecting Conditions

The first step in planning a screening effort is to evaluate and select those conditions which will benefit from screening. The following six criteria should be considered in this evaluation. The first criteria is that the condition should be treatable or controllable. Although this seems very obvious, it can cause a great deal of controversy such as in the question of screening for sickle cell anemia in the black population. A less controversial area, but one which is on some recommended screening lists, is color blindness. Although neither color blindness nor sickle cell anemia are treatable in a direct way, many people feel there are valid reasons for screening for them. It is up to the individual practitioner to decide whether the condition is one which will justify a screening effort in his or her particular screening situation.

Once you have established that a given condition is treatable, you must determine whether early treatment will help. This leads to the second criterion for determining whether a condition will benefit from screening: early treatment of a condition must improve the outcome of the condition more than treatment given at the usual time. If it doesn't, one might as well wait until the usual time of detection. To explain this further, we must consider the progression of a handicapping condition. In this progression from the onset to the final outcome, there is an optimal time when treatment will be more effective than any other time. Because symptoms of chronic conditions are often not obvious at the early critical stages, the optimal time often occurs before the usual time of diagnosis and treatment. Screening is done in order to move up the time of diagnosis to an earlier stage of the disease so treatment can begin when it is most effective. For those conditions where moving up the diagnosis and treatment does not improve the outcome, screening has little value. One example of this is juvenile diabetes, a condition in which the prognosis is not improved by starting treatment during the asymptomatic stage of the disease.

The third criterion is screening time: the length of time available between the point that a condition can be detected through screening and the optimal time to treat. In phenylketonuria (PKU), an inborn error of metabolism, this time period is only five weeks. It starts during the first week of life and lasts until a maximum of six weeks of age. If treatment is to be effective, it must be accomplished within a period of five weeks. In amblyopia, a vision problem, screening time should be adequate to allow detection of the condition before optimal treatment time passes. This depends upon the age of the patient and how often the practitioner intends to screen.

The fourth criterion is that a firm diagnosis should be possible in order to differentiate a disease from a borderline or a non-diseased individual. If diagnostic tests cannot accurately confirm the results of the screening, then the screening itself cannot be very accurate. Sometimes it is difficult to achieve a definite diagnosis because of problems in diagnostic measurement. For instance, even with their most elaborate equipment, audiologists occasionally have difficulty in diagnosing hearing loss in neonates. This is one of the reasons that several professional organizations recommend that hearing screening should not be routinely administered to newborn infants.

The fifth criterion concerns prevalence, the frequency with which a given condition is found in the population being screened. Except in rare instances, the condition should be relatively prevalent to justify the cost of screening for it. If 20,000 children were screened for a relatively prevalent condition, such as mental retardation, which has a prevalence rate of 3 percent, you would discover approximately 600 children with the condition, a significant number of cases. If you decided to screen the same number of children for a rare condition such as phenylketonuria, which has a prevalence rate of .005 percent, you would be likely to find only one case. The screening cost for the detection of rare conditions is therefore relatively high and can only be justified on the basis of very marked improvement as a result of early treatment and very damaging effects if the condition is left untreated, such as the case with phenylketonuria. If a condition is extremely prevalent, such as dental disease in some populations where it can be as high as 70 percent, it may not be efficient to spend time screening at all. Rather the money and effort could be used more effectively when directed toward immediate diagnosis and treatment.

Finally, criterion six is that the condition should be serious or potentially so. The seriousness of a condition, such as phenylketonuria, which can result in severe mental retardation if not treated before the child is one month old, is obviously an important factor in determining whether resources should be spent on screening for that condition. The question of seriousness, however, involves more than just the physiological damage to the child. It also involves the effect the condition has on the child's total development. For example, some people believe that speech problems in preschoolers are not serious enough to warrant treatment. However, when the child enters school with speech patterns which are significantly inappropriate for his age, his communication problems may be compounded with emotional and psychological problems. Implications that the condition might have for the family or the total community also influence the decision regarding seriousness. Although this criterion may seem elementary, you will find that deciding whether a condition is serious enough to justify the cost of screening for it is perhaps one of the most difficult and subjective decisions to make.

This completes the list of six criteria for evaluating and selecting conditions which benefit from screening. The condition must be treatable or controllable; early treatment must improve the outcome; screening time must be adequate; a firm diagnosis must be possible; the condition should be relatively prevalent; and the condition should be serious.

Criteria for Selecting Procedures

Once it is decided that a condition will benefit from screening, the next step is to evaluate the screening procedures. Only then can one determine how reasonable it will be to screen for that condition. One of the criteria is that the screening test used must be valid or accurate. That is, in most cases the suspicions of the screening test should be largely confirmed by the diagnosis. Validity affects the number of children referred for diagnosis and treatment. If the screening test is not valid, there will be a large number of abnormal children missed or normal children needlessly referred. Rarely will a test achieve 100 percent accuracy. One has to decide what is an acceptable level, and this depends on how many errors can be tolerated or afforded in each case. The screening procedures must also be quick and simple to administer. The purpose of screening is defeated if the test becomes too long or complicated to administer since screening implies a rapid application of tests to a large number of asymptomatic people. It is important that screening procedures be accepted by specialists who will be doing the follow-up. There should be agreement on which conditions would be identified and on the screening tests to be used. Parents and the local community should accept the procedures used when screening is done in large public programs. An example of a screening procedure which suffers for lack of public acceptance is the procedure for detecting rectal cancer in adults. Screening should not harm the individual being screened physically, psychologically, emotionally, or financially. For example, the sickle cell screening effort has been criticized because the stigma attached to the condition may limit available jobs and increase the cost of insurance premiums. Although no physical harm is involved in the screening, the labeling alone may be damaging. In all screening situations, extreme care should be taken not to label a child "abnormal" solely on the basis of a screening test.

Follow-up facilities should be available for diagnosis and treatment for those children who fail the screening test. Informing people that they might have a condition without being able to provide diagnostic and treatment services creates undue anxiety without benefiting the patient in question. In those cases where the purpose of screening is to demonstrate the need for additional diagnostic and treatment services, the people being screened should be informed of this purpose beforehand to avoid false expectations.

Up to this point, we have presented eleven of the twelve screening criteria. The twelfth criterion is treated separately even though it is directly affected by all the others; it concerns one of the most important areas of screening—cost benefits. There are always limited resources available whether they involve manpower, facilities, or money. It is important to distribute these resources so that the greatest benefit can be received for the cost involved. Therefore, for a screening effort to justify an investment of resources, screening costs must be reasonable. A cost benefit analysis must include a knowledge of all direct costs, many of which are often overlooked in determining the costs of screening. The costs to be considered include: cost of collecting a specimen, initial cost of equipment, depreciation, maintenance, consumable supplies, recording screening results, diagnostic follow-up, and treatment. Total cost of test administration should also be considered. This includes training, performance, and interpretation, as well as quality control and monitoring the administration to insure a high level of reliability. If paraprofessionals are able to administer a test proficiently under professional supervision, the cost can be substantially reduced. All of the direct costs of screening plus the number of children affected, the seriousness of the condition, and all other related criteria must be weighed against the cost of not detecting a case until the patient presents himself with symptoms.

The twelfth criterion for evaluating the procedures for screening completes our list. In summary, the tests must be valid or accurate, procedures simple, procedures accepted, screening harmless, follow-up available, and screening costs reasonable.

Examples

To put these criteria in a more realistic context, let's briefly look at two of the chronic conditions commonly recommended for screening, the first of which is amblyopia. As this condition is presented, notice which criteria are discussed. Amblyopia is impaired vision in one eye because of lack of use. There are two major causes of amblyopia, strabismus and refractive error. Strabismus, non-straight, crossed, or wall eyes, is a condition in which one eye looks at the object. The other eye may be turned in or out, up or down. Therefore, the brain receives two different images. Consequently, in the early stages of strabismus, the child sees double.

The other cause of amblyopia is refractive error in one eye whereby both eyes look at the object but only one focuses clearly. In this case, the child sees a blurred image with one eye and a clear image with the other. In both cases, at least two somewhat different images are received by the brain. To eliminate confusion, the brain learns to ignore images from the weaker eye, a practice which results in the non-use of that eye and possible blankness. Treatment may involve covering the stronger eye and forcing the weaker eye to be used, adding corrective lenses, or in a few cases, surgery. The earliest time that amblyopia can be detected through screening varies with the cause and the severity of the predisposing factors. For instance, severe strabismus may be identified before the child is one year old, whereas mild refractive error may not be identified until he is three or four years of age.

Optimal time to treat also varies with severity. As a result, screening time for amblyopia varies from two to five years. This is ample time for diagnosing and treating the condition prior to the time when treatment becomes less effective. If treated early enough, amblyopia may be reversed and a normal level of vision (or at least a better level) restored——provided the reflex patterns of vision have not yet become completely fixed in the developing child. Although there is some controversy over the exact age at which treatment should be provided, it is generally agreed that successful treatment is difficult if not started before five years of age. After eight years of age, treatment is mostly cosmetic.

Amblyopia is a relatively prevalent condition which approximately one out of every fifty children has or will develop. Unfortunately, the condition is one which cannot be detected through cursory observation. Since this is the case and the diagnostic costs would prohibit referring to identify the high risk population, there are brief, valid screening procedures available which use inexpensive materials to detect amblyopia as well as other visual problems. For example, one of the measures involves using a spinning toy or other novel items with children from six months to two and one-half years of age to evaluate the child's ability to follow an object. Another procedure is the Allen picture card test which screens for refractive error in children two years and older. A similar test for refractive error is the Snellen E chart used with children three years and older.

A procedure used to detect strabismus is the Corneal or Pupillary Light Reflection Test. This involves having the child look directly into a flashlight and observing a reflection from the child's cornea. The test may be used with children as young as six months. With adequate training and supervision, these tests may be administered by paramedical personnel under the supervision of professionals who are knowledgeable about the procedures.

Although this presentation of amblyopia was extremely brief, it should be relatively clear that the condition can benefit from screening. It is treatable; early treatment improves outcome; screening time is adequate; firm diagnosis is possible; the condition is relatively prevalent; and the condition is serious. But is screening for this condition practical? In evaluating the procedures discussed, the question can only be partially answered. The tests are valid; the procedure is simple; and the screening is harmless. The remaining criteria, which depend upon local circumstances, however, state that procedures must be accepted, follow-up available, and screening costs reasonable.

A different type of chronic condition of concern to those interested in the total development of the child is mental retardation.Many controversies exist regarding this condition, but it is generally agreed that it is important to detect any retarded development in a child as early as possible. One problem that faced the health worker for decades was the difficulty of defining mental retardation. Various definitions have been tried and debated. Some emphasize the genetic aspect, others the environmental. In 1973, the American Association of Mental Deficiency recommended the currently recognized definition. This definition refers to mental retardation as significant, subaverage intellectual functioning which exists concurrently with defects in adaptive behavior and is manifested during the developmental period between birth and eighteen years. "Significantly subaverage" refers to performance which is two or more standard deviations below the mean or average on an I.Q. test (which is below an I.Q. of seventy on the test represented by the graph on page 91). Adaptive behavior refers to how well an individual adapts to the personal and social standards appropriate for his age and cultural group.

The prevalence of mental retardation is approximately 3 percent, a significant percentage. Screening time for mental retardation is difficult to establish because of the varied etiologies involved. Generally it ranges from a few weeks to two years. Mental retardation due to progressive conditions such as phenylketonuria and galactosemia varies from a few weeks to a

SIGNIFICANT SUBAVERAGE
INTELLECTUAL FUNCTIONING

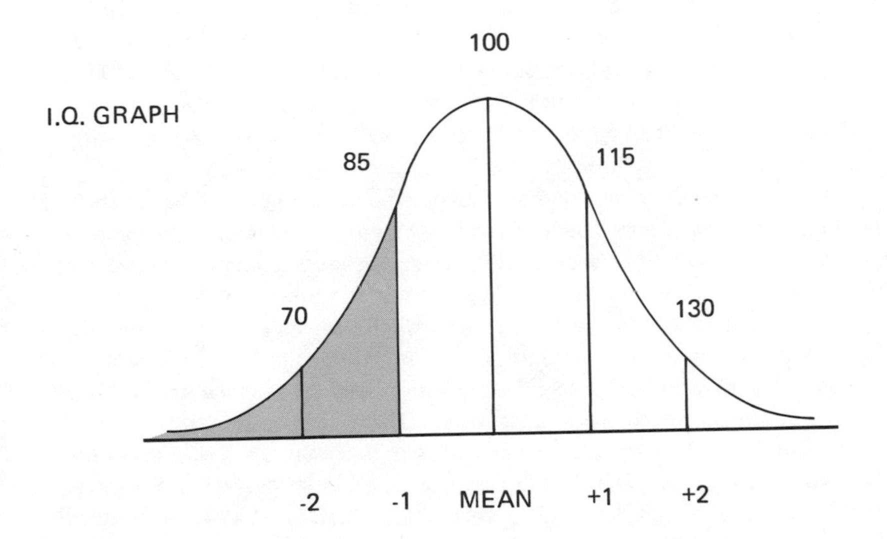

month or so, whereas the screening time for non-progressive types of retardation may be as long as one to two years. Through early intervention, it is often possible to minimize and occasionally prevent the handicapping effects of mental retardation. Unfortunately, the condition which can be identified as early as six months or younger is usually not identified until the child experiences difficulty in school.

Treatment may be specific (such as thyroid medication and preventing cretinism, special diet for enzyme abnormalities, physical therapy for neurological impairments, and environmental modifications for maternal deprivation). Non-specific treatment might include stimulus enrichment, special education, parental counseling, and treatment designed to minimize the development of secondary emotional problems in the child. One way to detect mental retardation at the earliest possible time is to screen periodically for significant delays in development. Any delays that are detected through screening can then be explored further through diagnostic evaluation. This screening should be done by using standard procedures of known accuracy and validity rather than relying on routine physical exams or developmental milestones.

The importance of this point has been emphasized in a number of studies which show that many pediatricians fail to detect a majority of the preschool children with I.Q.'s below 70. One procedure commonly used for detecting developmental delays during infancy and preschool is the Denver Developmental Screening Test. The test, which uses inexpensive materials, is administered by asking the child to perform various tasks appropriate for his age. These tasks are categorized in four sectors: personal-social, fine motor-adaptive, language, and gross motor. If the child does not perform a significant number of age-appropriate tasks in these areas, he is referred for diagnostic testing. The DDST is not an I.Q. test, but in several validity studies it has shown a high degree of accuracy in detecting children with I.Q.'s under 70. The test was standardized on a cross-sectional sample of over 1,000 Denver preschool children. The test requires ten to twenty minutes for administration. It can be given by paraprofessional personnel after special training.

Another screening instrument useful with children of up to eighteen months of age is the Developmental Screening Inventory or DSI. This tool consists of the systematic application of items in each of five areas: adaptive, gross motor, fine motor, language, and personal and social skills. A level of function in these areas can be made which correlates highly with the maturity age assigned on the basis of a complete diagnostic examination. The inventory requires a greater level of sophistication among evaluators than other screening approaches and was designed primarily for those well trained in the evaluation of development in infants and toddlers. It could be integrated easily into regular examining operations of health and educational professionals.

On the basis of the information you've just been presented, you can see that mental retardation is a condition which would benefit from screening. In evaluating the procedures discussed, however, we find that the information is not complete without knowing more about the local situation, particularly in regard to community acceptance, availability of follow-up facilities, and costs.

Amblyopia and mental retardation are two examples of chronic conditions which can meet most of the screening criteria. There are many others which do not. The point is that the central idea of early detection and treatment is essentially simple. However, the steps involved in accomplishing it are not, even though they appear deceptively easy. Screening is a powerful and effective tool, provided the screening effort is realistically planned and carefully evaluated.

Discussion

Q. Do you consider in your screening programs the seriousness or the consequences of making a mistake?

A. Yes. Screening requires the selection of a cutting point to separate the presumptive positives from the negatives. The selection of the cutting point should be on the basis of the relative costs of over and under referrals.

Q. Many people are using screening results as a plea (with legislators, etc.) for treatment services. If I can find numerous cases of a particular condition by screening a population, then aren't the screening results a rationale for requesting treatment resources?

A. As you remember, screening is the *presumptive* identification of diseases in handicapped children. While screening does not take the place of exacting diagnostic procedures, screening results are often useful in documenting the need for diagnostic procedures. If one knows the accuracy of screening results, one can estimate the number of children with the diagnosis in question and the subsequent need for treatment. It is incorrect to request treatment services on the basis of screening procedures of unknown validity since a screening test which is inaccurate will not provide accurate data on the number of children requiring treatment.

Q. If you wanted to screen for learning disabilities, how would you do it?

A. If screening school-aged children, I would ask the teachers to do the screening. If screening preschool-aged children, I would attempt to screen for conditions that have been documented to produce learning problems and for conditions that meet the disease criteria discussed previously. Initially, I would screen for problems affecting general development, hearing, vision, and school readiness. When to screen and how to screen for these types of problems is discussed in our book *Pediatric Screening Tests* which is edited by Frankenburg and Cany and published by Charles C. Thomas and Co.

Q. Who should have responsibility for the screening program you have discussed?

A. Ideally, screening should be performed by those people who are in the best position to screen the children and to obtain an appropriate follow-up service.

In the majority of cases, children are first seen by health care providers, such as physicians and nurses, who have screened children for many years. *EPSDT* is but one of these programs. It is important that one only screen for conditions which will be treated. Therefore, if screening is to be provided by the health profession, it should be in concert with the educational system so that children requiring remedial educational services will receive those services.

Q. What are some other screening programs?

A. The National Society for the Prevention of Blindness has a sound program. They have been training people to do vision screening for many years. For instance, they worked with the state health department in Michigan; with their assistance, Michigan has done an excellent job in screening children for visual defects. In the state of Minnesota, the society organized a large scale vision and hearing screening program. Both the Michigan and Minnesota programs have been well organized, and both have had good training programs for the volunteers who did the screening. State health departments (particularly the maternal and child health divisions) as well as social rehabilitation services at the state level should also be contacted for information on state screening programs. If you are thinking of beginning a screening program, the following questions will help you in conceptualization.

1. What kinds of handicapping conditions do you intend to identify? List them by the age groups you are planning to screen.

2. Who is presently conducting a screening program for the children listed under (1)?

3. What techniques or procedures will you use and what are your referral criteria?

4. Who is going to do the diagnostic work-up on all the suspect cases?

5. Who is going to provide the follow-up medical treatment? (e.g., glasses, hearing aids)?

6. Who will do the educational assessments? (It's important to differentiate assessment and diagnosis from screening. Screening is a quick and simple tool to identify suspect cases. Diagnostic tests are to confirm or disconfirm the suspicions.)

Q. Will you define screening, diagnosis, and assessment for educational purposes?

A. Screening is the application of simple, quick, and accurate tests or procedures to large masses of asymptomatic people to select those individuals who have a high likelihood of harboring the disease or handicap in question. Diagnosis is the process of taking a history and applying tests or procedures to determine if the person has the disease or handicap. The diagnostic process is generally much more time consuming, finite, and accurate, and it generally requires professional judgment. For these reasons, the diagnostic process is generally more expensive than the screening process. The educational assessment is generally perceived as a process of identifying the levels of function——such as the stage of developing number concepts, time concepts, and reading skills——as well as determining how this child learns in a given situation. Such information is often gathered through the use of criterion referenced tests that are extremely useful to the teacher in deciding what to teach and how to teach it.

Q. What about coordinating programs?

A. It is important to bring together all of the people who are involved in any of the stages we have discussed here. People from the state health department, the medical society, the welfare department, the local speech and hearing association, education, and other interested groups need to get together and talk about how they're going to coordinate their programs. They need––as a group––to decide who's going to be doing screening and who's going to answer the questions that have been asked throughout this chapter. Only when such programs are coordinated at the community level can a plan be properly coordinated.

Further Considerations

The following questions should prove helpful in developing or assessing a screening program in your state. Your responses to the questions should be organized according to the ages of the children to be served: birth to eighteen months, eighteen months to thirty-six months, three and four years, and five, six, and seven years.

1. Define the geographic area to be served. Example: the entire state, a county, several counties.

2. What kinds and degrees of handicapping conditions do you intend to identify?

3. Who is presently screening children for the conditions you listed under number 2?

4. What techniques are being employed in your screening effort? What referral criteria are being used for finding children to be screened, and who pays for the screening?

5. Who does the diagnostic work-up for suspect cases, and who pays?

6. Who provides follow-through medical treatment?

7. Who conducts educational assessments, and what instruments are used? Who pays?

8. Who provides educational service for the young handicapped child, and who pays?

APPENDICES

APPENDIX A

Legislation for Handicapped Children

Since 1969, when Public Law 91-230 (Title VI, Elementary and Secondary Education Act Amendments) was enacted to provide federal support for handicapped children, several pieces of legislation—which expand the original law—have been passed. In this section, the salient features of recent legislation, which is explicitly for or which includes handicapped children, are reviewed.

Public Law 91-230 (Title VI) "The Elementary and Secondary Education Act Amendments"

"Part A, General Provisions." This law went into effect in 1969. It was subsequently amended in 1974 by Public Law 93-280 (known as "The Education Amendments of 1974") and in 1975 by Public Law 94-142 (known as "Education for All Handicapped Children Act of 1975"). The General Provisions of the law did three important things. They defined handicapped children as "mentally retarded, hard of hearing, deaf, speech impaired, visually handicapped, seriously emotionally disturbed, crippled, or other health impaired children who by reason thereof require special education and related services." They defined children with learning disabilities as "those children who have a disorder in one or more of the basic psychological processes involved in understanding or in using language, spoken or written which disorder may manifest itself in imperfect ability to listen, think, speak, read, write, spell, or do mathematical calculations. Such disorders include such conditions as perceptual handicaps, brain injury, minimal brain dysfunction, dyslexia, and developmental aphasia. Such term does not

include children who have learning problems which are primarily the result of visual, hearing, or motor handicaps, or mental retardation, or emotional disturbance, or environmental disadvantage." Finally, the General Provisions established the Bureau of Education for the Handicapped.

"Part B, Handicapped Preschool and School Programs." The law also made possible grant assistance to states for education of handicapped children. In order to receive funds, each state was required to submit a "state plan." The plan had to explain how the funds would be used for the "initiation, expansion, or improvement of programs and projects" for handicapped children. Federal dollars were in no case to be used in place of the state, local, or private funds that would otherwise have been used for educating the children.

"Part C, Handicapped Children's Early Education Program." This part of the law authorized funds to public and private non-profit agencies for establishing and operating model early education projects for the handicapped. Each project is to serve a particular local population. Each is also expected to seek funding sources which will support the project or its program when the three years of government funding is terminated. All of the projects are to develop programs which can be used, in whole or in part, by others serving handicapped children. A local contribution of 10 percent of the total project cost is required during the first three years of funding.

Public Law 93-380
"The Education Amendments of 1974"

This law significantly amended 91-230 in several ways. First, it required state plans: (1) to include the goal of "providing full educational opportunities to all handicapped children," (2) to develop plans for using funds to achieve the goal, and (3) to place priority on serving handicapped children not receiving services. The law also included certain clauses designed to protect the population to be served.

(1) Due process guarantees were established to insure that the parents or guardians were aware of and agreed with any changes in their child's educational placement.

(2) A least restrictive clause was included so that handicapped children would be placed in an environment that was as close to that of non-handicapped children as possible.

For 1976, Public Law 93-380 further amended requirements for the plan. All states were to include procedures for identifying all children in need of special educational and related services. Data on children was to be kept confidential, and a timetable for providing educational services to all children was to be included in the plan.

Public Law 94-142
"Education for All Handicapped Children Acts of 1975"

Regulations to guide the application of this law have not yet been developed by the Bureau of Education for the Handicapped. Consequently, at this point, any or all interpretations of the law's meaning may prove to be inaccurate. The information presented here merely describes the contents of the law's various sections. The law has two major parts. Part A contains the general provisions and these provisions are elaborated in Sections 601 through 607. Part B contains the assistance for education of all handicapped children. This assistance is elaborated in Sections 611 through 620.

Part A. Part A, Section 601, contains the findings and purpose of the act. In general, the findings are that children are not receiving full and appropriate services, that service technology has reached the level where it is possible to provide appropriate services, that state and local agencies have the responsibility to provide educational services but present financial resources are inadequate to meet the special education needs of handicapped children. The general purposes of the act are to ensure that all handicapped children have a free public education with related services to meet their "unique" needs, ensure that the rights of parents and children are protected, to assist states and local education agencies, and to assess and ensure the effectiveness of efforts to educate handicapped children.

Section 602 of Part A contains the crucial definitions of the act. These definitions include: (1) special education, (2) related services, (3) free appropriate public education, (4) individualized education programs, (5) excess costs, (6) native language, and (7) intermediate educational unit.

Sections 603 through 607 contain various provisions of the act. For example, Section 604 establishes a national advisory committee for handicapped children and Section 607 establishes grants to remove architectural barriers.

Sections 608 through 610 are not included in this act.

Part B. Section 611, "Entitlements and Allocations," specifies the formula to be used for determining the funds each state will receive under

94-142. The general formula is: the number of handicapped children, aged three through twenty-one, in a state multiplied by a percentage of the average per pupil expenditure in public elementary and secondary schools in the U.S. The percentages are as follows: 5 percent in 1978; 10 percent in 1979; 20 percent in 1980; 30 percent in 1981; and 40 percent in 1982. The Section includes a definition of "per pupil expenditure" and the way in which it will be determined. It also specifies the agencies to be given money in the state and places a limit on the amount of funds that may be used for administrative costs incurred in implementing the provision of Sections 612 and 613.

Section 612, "Eligibility," explains how a state may become eligible to receive funds under 94-142. Essentially, it must have a policy that assures all handicapped children the right to a free appropriate public education. The state must develop a description of the kind and number of facilities, services, and people that will be needed in the state to meet the goal of "free appropriate education . . ." It must reach this goal for the three through eighteen age group by 1978 and for the three through twenty-one age group by 1980 (unless state law prohibits serving the three through five and eighteen through twenty-one age groups). It must develop a plan for identifying, locating, and evaluating all children in the state who are handicapped, and it must develop a "practical method for finding who is and who is not served." Each local education agency or other intermediate agency must maintain records on each handicapped child served. Finally, the state must assure that in carrying out the requirements of the Section, a process will be established in which parents of handicapped children and others involved in or concerned with education for such children are routinely consulted.

Section 613, "State Plans," specifies that funds allowed under this act are to be used to provide free appropriate education to all handicapped children and that the state must include in its plan a system of personnel development and in-service training of special educational and support personnel so that all personnel necessary to carry out the purposes of this act are appropriately and adequately trained and prepared. States must also include, in the plans, procedures which will ensure that 94-142 funds are not inappropriately used. A provision for reporting to the commissioner on the use of funds and for keeping records on the use of funds must be included. Procedures for evaluating, "at least" annually, the effectiveness of programs in meeting the needs of handicapped children and an advisory panel to the state (made up of teachers, handicapped adults, parents of handicapped children, local education agency officials, etc.) to advise on unmet needs, state policies, and so on, must be included in the plan.

Section 614, "Application," specifies that the local education agency or intermediate educational unit desiring payments under Section 611 must submit an application to the state education agency which provides assurances that the money will be used for excess costs incurred in meeting the goal of providing education for all handicapped children in their service area. These costs may be attributable to such things as identification and evaluation programs, personnel development programs, facilities, etc. This part also contains information on the ways local education agencies must be accountable for use of the fund and on the relationships between the local education agencies and state education agencies in terms of reviewing applications, accepting or rejecting applications, etc.

Section 615, "Procedural Safeguards," specifies the methods that state and local agencies must use to assure that handicapped children and their parents or guardians are guaranteed procedural safeguards with respect to the provision of free appropriate public education by such agencies and units. These include such things as allowing parents to see records of their handicapped child. This Section also specifies the procedures to be used when a complaint is received as well as the rights of the complaintant.

Section 616, "Withholding and Judicial Review," concerns the actions to be taken by the commissioner when failure of a state education agency to comply with Section 612 or Section 613 has been established.

Section 617, "Administration," explains the duties of the commissioner. He is authorized to provide technical assistance to the states relating to their accomplishment of the provisions of 94-142, to provide short term training institutes as necessary, to disseminate information, and to insure that states provide certification of the actual number of handicapped children within one year of 94-142's enactment. He is also directed to provide a uniform financial report to be used by state education agencies in submitting state plans. The secretary is authorized to take appropriate action to protect the confidentiality of "any personally identifiable data." Finally, the commissioner is authorized to hire personnel to conduct data collection and evaluation activities as outlined in Section 618.

Section 618, "Evaluation," directs the commissioner to measure and evaluate the impact of the program authorized under this part and the effectiveness of state efforts to assure free appropriate education for all handicapped children. The commissioner is also directed to conduct a number of statistical studies, such as the number of handicapped children in each state. He must also provide for the evaluation of programs by developing methods and procedures for evaluation. Finally, he must submit a report to Congress each year which includes evaluation findings and recommendations.

Section 619, "Incentive Grants," authorizes the commissioner to grant to any state, which has satisfied the requirements of Sections 612 and 613 and which has applied for the incentive grant, three hundred dollars for each child (aged three to five inclusive) who receives special education and related services and is counted for the purposes of Section 611.

Section 620, "Payments," authorizes the commissioner to make payments to each state in amounts which the state education agency of each state is eligible to receive. The commissioner is also directed one year after enactment of the law to establish specific criteria for determining whether a particular disorder or condition may be considered a specific learning disability for purposes of designating children with specific learning disabilities; he is also directed to establish regulations for diagnostic procedures for specific learning disabilities; and to establish monitoring procedures to make sure states are complying with the criteria established.

Public Law 92-424 (1972)
Head Start, as amended by the "Economic Opportunity, Community Partnership Act of 1974"

The amended version of this law stipulates: "not less than 10 percentum of the total enrollment opportunities in each state in the Head Start program shall be available for handicapped children." Even if Congress fails to appropriate the funds necessary for meeting this requirement, the state Head Start programs are still responsible for having a 10 percent handicapped enrollment.

The amended version of the law explicitly defines (in the same way as 91-230) what it means by handicapped to prevent programs from labeling children for the sole purpose of meeting the quota; and it defines speech problems to prevent programs from labeling children from different cultural/ethnic environments as handicapped.

Congress appropriated twenty million dollars in fiscal year 1975 to help meet the added costs of serving handicapped clients. The Office of Child Development—which has responsibility for administering the act—identified nine areas in which the money could be spent:

1. Outreach, recruitment and enrollment
2. Screening, assessment, and professional diagnosis
3. Direct provision or purchase (when not available on a donated basis) of needed special education, other special services, and therapy
4. Cost of additional full-time or part-time Head Start staff
5. Purchase or lease of special equipment and materials
6. Modification of physical facilities
7. Pre-service and in-service staff training

8. Development of core capability
9. Funding of summer Head Start services to handicapped children

Public Law 93-647
"The Social Service Amendment of 1974"

This law was designed to encourage states to provide services "directed at the goal of:

1. achieving or maintaining economic self-support to prevent, reduce, or eliminate dependency,
2. achieving or maintaining self-sufficiency, including reduction or prevention of dependency,
3. preventing or remedying neglect, abuse, or exploitation of children and adults unable to protect their own interests, or preserving, rehabilitating or reuniting families,
4. preventing or reducing inappropriate institutional care by providing for community-based care, home-based care, or other forms of less intensive care, or
5. securing referral or admission for institutional care when other forms of care are not appropriate, or providing services to individuals in institutions."

The government places few restrictions on the ways the social services money is used by each state as long as the state plan focuses on the above goals. Consequently, the amount of social services money each state spends on early childhood education for the handicapped varies.

APPENDIX B

A Review of the Literature for Developers of State Plans

The information in this rationale is intended to help program developers formulate rationales for early childhood education programs in their states. The information, which is presented in question and answer format, should be viewed in light of the following:

1. What groups within your state would be likely to pose such questions?

2. How would the groups ask the questions?

3. Would the suggested responses satisfy the groups?

4. If not, what additional information would need to be supplied?

A. Why does a state education agency need a rationale for early intervention for young, handicapped children?

A rationale is needed to provide data to support your request for funds to provide services to handicapped children and their families. The rationale is also a means of making various interest groups aware of your activities.

B. What is the population to be informed by an early childhood education rationale?

It is anyone who can potentially be helpful in developing early childhood programs. Primarily, these groups are advocacy, funding, and service delivery agencies.

Potential advocacy agencies include groups responsible (1) for identifying children needing service, (2) for making service available to children, and (3) for advocating more services in the appropriate agencies. Such groups include the informed public, parents, action groups (child advocacy, associations for handicapped children, church groups, etc.) and selected consultative personnel (medical, university, etc.).

Funding agencies (and those groups directly influencing such agencies) include state governments (governor, legislative bodies, elected officials, and various departments of government) and certain private organizations (foundations, associations, etc.).

Service delivery groups are directly responsible for offering educational assistance to handicapped children. They include state departments of public instruction; school administrators at the state, regional or local level; teachers and teacher organizations; and private educational facilities offering care for young handicapped children.

C. What trends in our society are bringing the issue of early childhood education to the forefront?

The literature points to developments in six areas.

1. In *education,* attitudes toward services for the handicapped have evolved from a "forget and hide" approach to a "screen and segregate" attitude to the present attitude of "identify and help" (Caldwell, 1973).

2. In *psychology,* there has been a revival of interest in the infant and early developmental period of life (e.g., Jean Piaget). Jensen

(1967) states, for example, "Our present knowledge of the development of learning abilities indicates that the preschool years are the most important years of learning in the child's life . . . and this learning is the foundation for all further learning" (p. 125).

3. In *politics,* the issue of poverty and its relationship with mental development has been implicated as a high risk factor (Gordon, 1968; Frost, 1975).

4. In the *legal arena:*

    a. The courts have ruled that handicapped children must receive education "suitable" to [their] abilities (Zedler, 1974).
    b. Nearly 70 percent of the states have laws which mandate education for the handicapped (Abeson, 1974).
    c. Some states have moved to allow children to enter school at birth.
    d. The National Education Association, the 1974 National Governors' Conference, and other groups have publically endorsed early education programs for the handicapped.
    e. The 1969 Elementary and Secondary Education Act Amendment, Title VI (Public Law 91-230), has made early education for the handicapped fiscally possible (Martin, LaVor, Bryan, Scheflin, 1970).
    f. The Economic Opportunity Act Amendment of 1972 required that 10 percent of Head Start program children be handicapped (Ackerman and Moore, in press).
    g. Establishment of the Bureau of Education for the Handicapped within the department of Health, Education, and Welfare, the Handicapped Children's Early Education Assistance Act (Martin, 1971), and the Model Center's Program (Olshin, 1971) have all made early education a prominent national issue.
    h. In the area of *parent power,* Ross, DeYoung, and Cohen (1971) point out that parents of the handicapped are exercising their legal options in the quest for services.

5. In the *social* area:

    a. Increases in the number of working women and the "women's rights" movement have increased the need for child care facilities in general.

b. Recognition of the strain that a handicapped child places on the family unit has also helped sustain arguments for early education. Forbes (1958) describes the dependency of a handicapped child in terms of "prolonged infancy." The continual responsibility to the handicapped child often creates frustration, strife, and confusion in the family (Carver and Carver, 1972; Ehlers, 1966; Jacobs, 1969; and Farber, 1959) which could be alleviated with early educational intervention and support to the family.

D. Why should a state become involved in an early childhood education program?

1. The primary factor is that early education programs benefit young handicapped children. Recent studies indicate that the best time to begin work with children is prior to school entry. By age eight, reports an HEW study, children have obtained 80 percent of their total adult intellectual capacity (Roos, 1974). "The best time to attack a child's mental or emotional handicap appears to be the period from birth through early childhood" (Roos, 1974, 1973). (Also see: Lillie, 1975.)

   Arthur Jensen (1967) states: " . . . it may be concluded that the nursery school years can greatly affect the later educability of the child. His long experiences during this crucial period of mental development will determine in no small measure how far he will successfully go in school and how far he will go in life" (p. 135).

   Following a survey of the literature concerning what effects experience might have on intelligence, J. McVicker Hunt (1961) made the following statements: "The assumption that intelligence is fixed and that its development is predetermined by the genes is no longer tenable" (p. 342); "It might be feasible to discover ways to govern the encounters that children have with their environments, especially during the early years of their development, to achieve a substantially faster rate of intellectual capacity" (p. 363). The issues that Frost (1975) feels are still to be explored include questions concerning the intensity and nature of the experiences used in the intervention programs.

   Bloom (1964) investigated the appropriateness of early intervention by examining fifty years of child development studies. He concluded that the studies "make it clear that intelligence is a developing function and that the stability of measured intelligence increased with age. Both types of data suggest that in terms of intelligence measured at age seventeen, about 50 percent of the development takes place between conception and age four" (1964, p. 88). He further states, "These results make it clear that a single early measure of general intelligence cannot be the basis for a long term decision about an individual" (p. 88).

Ausubel (1964) suggests that the severity of a child's developmental problems should be used to guage the intensity and length of intervention. If a child has a language problem, for example, intervention should be intense enough and long term enough to prevent the problem from affecting the child's later school experiences. [Additional discussion of this topic can be found under Question E.]

2. There are secondary factors for a state's involvement in early intervention.

    a. *Legal.* State and Supreme Court rulings have called for the equal education of all children (Abeson, 1974a; Ross, DeYoung, and Cohen, 1971). Zedler (1974) interprets these rulings to mean that each child should receive education which is appropriate for his abilities. If a state fails to provide appropriate education, parents may use legal means to obtain necessary services for their children.
    b. *Social.* In addition to the social factors listed in the answer to Question C, Forbes (1958) discusses social factors that suggest the time is right for state programs:
        (1) The growing number of teen-aged mothers also increases the number of children who are likely to be high risk as well as suffer from abuse and neglect.
        (2) Medicine has made possible the survival of many premature infants. These babies have a greater risk of central nervous system damage, brain damage, mental retardation, malnutrition, and motor and language skill development difficulties.
    c. *Economic.* When considering economic reasons for early intervention, it is best to begin by considering the cost of education in general. Then, the cost of early treatment programs compared to the cost of the educational and social problems that can often be prevented through early treatment should be explored.

(1) *General Information.* Special education generally costs more than regular education because it entails providing educational experiences in an environment that is more restrictive than the environment in which regular education is conducted. For example, Frohreich (1973) found that physically handicapped, emotionally disturbed, and visually impaired children require an environment with a greater adult-child ratio than regular education and that such children have certain prosthetic requirements which boost costs. The cost of special education, of course, depends on the severity of the handicap. Figures from a small sample of Handicapped Early Education Program (HCEEP) projects show annual costs range from $700/child (home-based, mild handicaps) to $4,000/child (center-based, moderate to severe handicaps). The average yearly cost per child is $1,800.

(2) *Educational Economics.* Hobbs (1975) cites studies that suggest long-term care of the handicapped may be reduced by early treatment programs. Weikart (1971), similarly, suggests that early help for a child may make it possible for that child to move into regular educational programs earlier than the child who receives no "early" assistance. In his study of the grade placements of five groups of children who participated in the Ypsilanti Perry Preschool Project (see question G), the following results were obtained:

Of the experimental children who received preschool educational experiences and later went to public school, 83 percent were participating in a regular class and achieving at expected grade level, 15 percent were in special educational placement, and 2 percent were over age in their grade placement. These figures may be contrasted with the control children who did not receive preschool education: 61 percent were in regular classes at the expected grade level, 24 percent were in special educational settings, and 15 percent were over age for their grade (indicating retainment in grade).

A child who was served by a regular educational setting annually received $260 from state funds and $600 from local funds resulting in an educational expense of $860 per normal child per year. Grade retainment, then, costs the funding agencies an extra $860 per retainment. For every experimental child who was retained in a grade, seven control children were retained. In terms of cost per 100 children, $12,900 was spent on the control group and $1,720 was spent on the experimental group beyond normal expenditures—simply because the children had to be retained in a grade.

Children who are eligible for special education placement receive additional state and county funds amounting to $800 per year. This means the experimental group received another $12,000 and the control group another $19,000 in educational funds. Weikart estimates the lifetime educational costs for the control children could run as high as $85,000.

Weikart states that children who have experienced preschool intervention are "better able to manage later school experiences as measured by capacity to proceed through school at regular grade placement and avoid special education services or retention-in-grade" (p. 11). There are obvious savings for the state educational funding agencies involved as well.

Similar results were reported in a longitudinal study conducted by Hodges, McCandless and Spicker (1971). In this study, disadvantaged mentally retarded children who received preschool intervention were more likely to remain in a regular class after entering public school than were comparable children who had not received such experience. In addition to intervention, preventive programs which include screening for potentially retarding or damaging conditions can also have large payoffs. Certain conditions present at birth or in the child's early environment may drastically alter his learning abilities if not detected early and prevented. For example, Scriver (1974) in a discussion of the cost benefits that early screening of potentially retarding diseases can yield, says: "We are pleased to find that one dollar spent for the screening and treatment of PKU [for example] is more than balanced by a saving of $4 in institutional and other care which would otherwise be given to non-screened, untreated, retarded PKU patients" (p. 617).

(3) *Labor Economics.* There is evidence that some handicaps, especially mild mental retardation, can be reversed if caught in time. For example, cultural-familial retardation or CFR (Giradeau, 1971) refers to disorders in which the individuals in a family experience retarded development without an observable biological basis. The I.Q. range for this kind of retardation is between 50 and 75. Zigler (1967) notes that CFR affects about 75 percent of the entire population of retarded individuals. Conley (1973) suggests, "a more stimulating environment [could enable] over half of the retarded to achieve I.Q. scores above the arbitrary cut off point [for mild retardation] of 70" (p. 321). He continues, "If all demographic groups had the same rate of mental retardation as exists among middle and upper class white children, the prevalence of mental retardation would decrease almost 80 percent. Unless one wishes to argue that there are important genetic differences among demographic groups with respect to intellectual potential, this represents the extent to which it is possible to prevent mental retardation. Much of the overall prevalence of mental retardation is probably due to cultural deprivation" (p. 302). The savings that would be made possible if all CFR were prevented are staggering. Conley (1973) states, " . . . a partial estimate of the social cost of mental retardation in 1970 was $7 billion. This included the productivity losses among retardates and the excess cost of services . . . (p. 239). The benefits of reducing cultural deprivation are large. If, in 1970, nonwhite men and women had the same unemployment rates and earning levels as whites, aggregate output would have increased by $21 billion. This loss reflects the influence of many factors and it is not possible to estimate, even crudely, the part of this loss that can be attributed solely to lowered I.Q. due to cultural conditions" (p. 321).

An excellent study of the prevention of CFR was conducted by Skeels and Dye in 1938-39. They subjected one group of retarded orphans to early environmental stimulation, and compared them to another group who received

no preschool assistance. Skeels (1966), in
study of the two groups of children aft
reached adulthood, found some rather dra
ences in occupational and earning levels: "the thirtee
subjects in the experimental group were all self-supporting and none were wards of any institution—public or private . . . . The occupational status of the eleven members of the contrast group was significantly different" (p. 32). Four from the contrast group were inmates in an institution, three were dishwashers, one was a drifter who had held various jobs, one worked part-time in a cafeteria, one was employed by an institution as a gardener's helper, and one was a clear occupational success.

Skeels also reported "striking differences in income between the experimental and contrast groups. The two unmarried women and one unskilled spouse in the experimental group who earned wages of $2,200 or less, the lowest in the group, still earned more than the lowest seven earners in the contrast group. Only one person in the contrast . . . earned more than the median of the experimental group" (p. 38).

Skeels also compared the two groups in terms of costs expended for institutional and rehabilitative care. "Up to the time of this follow-up study, the thirteen children in the experimental group had spent a total of seventy-two years and five months in institutional residence, at a total cost of $30,716.01, whereas the twelve children in the contrast group had spent a total of 273 years in residence, at a total cost of $138,571.68" (1966, p. 43). Estimates of the amount of federal income taxes paid by the two groups for 1963 reveal that for the experimental group, combined income was $62,498 and taxes were approximately $5,485. The contrast group's combined income was $19,826—with taxes approximately $2,238.

E. What evidence do we have that early childhood education does in fact make a positive difference in the development of a child?

In this response, we will explore five aspects of the intervention effectiveness issue.

1. *The Child.* Gordon (1968) suggests that a number of things we know about development makes it possible to evaluate the effectiveness of early intervention programs. We know that infants develop sight and hearing abilities at a relatively early age. We know that children do not merely passively react to incoming stimuli: they appear to be motivated intuitively to explore their environment. Finally, we know that both nature (heredity) and nurture (environment) play important roles in individual child development; environment is a variable which can be manipulated by the educator. [See also Hunt, 1961; O'Connor, 1975; Cooper and Zubek, 1958; Thompson and Heron, 1954; Sackett, 1967; and Beach, 1966.]

2. *The Environment.* The 1966 Coleman Report (O'Connor, 1975), an inspection of the United States system of education, indicates that many lower socio-economic status children fall significantly below national averages, even at the first grade level, in school achievement. By grade 12 there is a total lag in achievement scores for minority groups. Coleman reported that schools appear to be ineffective in helping the child who is already disadvantaged, for whatever reasons, to overcome this initial deficit.

   Other evidence that "an enriched environment" positively affects the development of abilities is offered by Kirk (1958). In a study of children between three and six years old who were moderately retarded, Kirk examined the effects of nursery school attendance or non-attendance on institutionalized and non-institutionalized children. Seventy percent of the children attending nursery school showed 10 to 30 I.Q. point gains (Caldwell, 1970). [See also: Skeels, 1966, as described in answer to Question D, (4c); Dennis, 1960; and Dennis and Najarian, 1957.]

   Studies by Rheingold and Bayley (1959) report that infants appear to receive more adult attention in the home than in an institution, and that an increase in the amount of adult attention appears to raise the degree of immediate social responsiveness in the children as well as to increase their abilities to develop speech skills following release from the institution. Heber, Dever, and Conry (1968) state that "studies of various socio-economic groups have shown that children from lower socio-economic groups score lower on intelligence tests than do children from higher socio-economic groups" (p. 7). Caldwell (1970) concludes, "differences on most cognitive variables can be demonstrated as a function of an early childhood spent in environments presumed to differ in the amount and quality of available stimulation" (p. 179).

3. *The Disadvantaged Environment.* Hess and Shipman (1965) analyzed the differences of behavior between mothers of the middle and lower classes. The two groups showed significant differences in teaching styles, mother's language, and methods of child control (Caldwell, 1970).

   Caldwell (1970) refers to a number of studies (Wortes, Bardach, Cutler and Freeman; Pavenstedt; and Malone) which indicate that "the interpersonal and experimental environment of the lower class child has been found to involve disorganization to the point of chaos and hostility or indifference to developmental needs" (p. 720).

4. *Early Childhood Project Results.* There have been a number of projects which have offered early educational ameliorative experiences to children of ages three to six. Perhaps a pioneer effort in the field is that of Susan Gray and Rupert Klaus (see Gray and Klaus, 1969; Gray, 1969; Klaus and Gray, 1968). This project, the Early Training Project, was begun in 1961. Four groups of preschool, low income, black children were involved in the study as experimental or control groups. The two experimental groups received intervention during the summer months for ten weeks—one group for three summers prior to first grade, one for two. Summer programs were supplemented during the rest of the year by weekly home visits by trained workers. In the seven year follow-up results, Gray (1969) reported that on the Binet intelligence test "the experimental groups have remained significantly superior to the control groups" (p. 4). Significant differences between test and subtest scores were maintained through grades one and two.

   Weikart (1971) reported (see also answer to Question D) that three-year-old children from disadvantaged backgrounds were given daily preschool experiences in a cognitively oriented setting for two years at the Ypsilanti Perry Preschool Project (see also Weikart, Deloria, Lawser, and Wiegerink, 1970). Teaching visits to the home were also carried out weekly. The effects of the preschool training were followed longitudinally as the children entered school. Initial findings indicated that I.Q. scores were significantly higher on the Stanford-Binet for the preschool training group than the control group. In grades one and three, the experimental children received higher achievement test scores. The preschool training group also was rated higher by teachers in terms of development in social, emotional and other academic areas. These ratings continued to be higher through grade three. Additional results showed a contrast in grade level attainment and the need for special education services between experimental and control groups.

Weikart (1967) also reported preliminary results of the Deutsch Preschool and Early Elementary Education Project (see Deutsch, 1962; 1968). In one phase of the project, experimental groups of disadvantaged four year olds participated in special preschool classes and then entered an enriched kindergarten setting. Results for one phase of children going through the program showed a five point I.Q. gain over two years for the experimental children and a seven point I.Q. loss for the controls. A second phase of children showed a similarly significant, though not as marked, trend.

Head Start is a federal attempt to provide preschool compensatory education to young disadvantaged children. The first summer it operated, Head Start served 561,000 children (Smith and Bissell, 1970). The first full year programs served 20,000 children. The centers offering Head Start programs throughout the nation have been autonomous to a large degree; and, therefore, the characteristics of the programs differ greatly, even as to the number of months that constitute a full time program. A number of questions about the claim that Head Start significantly bettered the cognitive functioning of participating children prompted the 1968 Westinghouse Learning Corporation and Ohio University evaluation of the outcomes of the Head Start effort. The preliminary results were not very encouraging in terms of longitudinal impact; the most optimistic findings indicated that full year programs had an influence on development in cognitive areas through grade three; the program appeared to have the most effect in traditionally disadvantaged areas (geographically); and parent participation and interest were good. Smith and Bissell (1970) reanalyzed the Westinghouse-Ohio University data, criticizing the research methodology in a number of areas. The results from their reanalyzation are most favorable.

> In a re-analysis of the effect of full-year Head Start on the overall sample of first-grade children, we found, unlike the Report, that the Head Start group scored higher than the control group on the Metropolitan Readiness Test by a large enough margin for us to consider the differences 'educationally significant' . . . . a re-analysis of data on urban black centers . . . led us to the conclusion that, at least for this sub-group, the Head Start experience is of clear educational importance (p. 101).

5. *The Age Factor in Intervention Studies.* In many of the previously reviewed studies and projects, early gains evident in the experimental preschool groups appeared to "wash out" by grades three or four. A key for understanding the reason behind this phenomena could lie in the timing of the intervention experiences. The studies offered services to the child from age three or older. It may be "that most United States studies of compensatory education for psychosocially disadvantaged children begin too late and provide too little" (Hodges, McCandless and Spicker, 1971, p. 9). It may be that in order to avoid a "wash out" of early gains and to prevent disadvantages or exceptionality from having lasting effects, early education programs should begin prior to age three, perhaps as early as birth (Caldwell, 1970; O'Connor, 1975).

Horowitz and Paden (1974) state, "the strong empirical evidence derived from normative studies has suggested that by the time a child reaches five years of age, his response characteristics on a variety of tasks begin to stabilize" (p. 338). Blank (1970), in a discussion of human behavior modifiability, states:

> There are . . . in almost all theories limitations to the degree of modifiability that can take place. In general, the major correlate for this limitation is age; that is, the older the organism, the less the change (p. 16).

Weikart (1967) refers to Bloom's (1964) thesis "that 50 percent of the intelligence measured at age seventeen is developed by age four" (p. 178). Weikart reports documentation by Pasamanick and Knoblock (1967) that deprivation may be evident as early as three years of age.

Caldwell (1970) in a summary of a number of studies (Golden and Birns, 1968; Hertzig, Birch, Thomas, and Mendiz, 1968; and Escalona and Corman, 1967) states that the research "points to the period of about eighteen months to three years as the time at which significant differences in cognitive level and style begin to appear between children from relatively privileged and underprivileged backgrounds" (p. 719).

> Weikart states: "It is reasonable to assume that: (1) The experiences provided by the environment to the disadvantaged child are inadequate for continued normal development after age one; and (2) The process of deprivation is probably insidious in that it deprives the child of key experiences necessary to establish the foundation for future development before the effects of the deprivation process are noticeable through performance tests (1967, p. 178).

F. What arguments can be advanced for early education programs for various kinds of handicapping conditions?

While most reasons given for early education are based on information available concerning high risk and disadvantages populations, there are important arguments from other areas of special education.

1. *Gifted.* Torrance (1974) places significant emphasis on recognizing and developing the individuality of children as a way of developing their gifts. Such emphasis, he feels, "must give full recognition to the fact that individuality is established largely in the early years of a child's life and that these early years are critically important in the emergence of a healthy, strong identity and the realization of potentialities" (1974, p. 190). Torrance believes that intervention should begin shortly after birth because, even then, the gifted child has begun to demonstrate differences from the norm. The implication of this view for early childhood educational stimulation programs for disadvantaged children who have a potential for giftedness but lack stimulation opportunities in the home is, perhaps, that the development of low creativity may correlate with an absence of proper intelligence. Giftedness may be particularly difficult to identify in children who are handicapped because of the attention given to the handicapping condition(s) or the effects of the condition on the child.

2. *Mentally Retarded.* Roos (1974) cites evidence to support his contention that, for retarded children, "programs of early education seem particularly crucial if the individual is to be given the opportunity of reaching maximum potential" (p. 243). Mental retardation may result from organic conditions present either pre-, peri-, or postnatally or as a result of what have been labeled "cultural-familial factors."

   a. *Organic Mental Retardation.* A number of organic disturbances may have lasting effects on a child's mental abilities. Among these are birth injuries, Down's Syndrome or mongolism, and untreated phenylketonuria. Taking Down's Syndrome as an example of an organic cause of retardation, Hayden and Haring (1974) cite figures by Smith and Wilson (1973) placing the occurrence of Down's Syndrome at one out of each 640 births. Although the intellectual effects of Down's Syndrome varies, Hayden and Haring report that "until fairly recently there was all too little speculation about the eventual mental prognosis for children born with Down's Syndrome: it was generally assumed to be poor" (p. 16). They further report that institutionalization has been, until recent times, the predominant prescription for treatment of this population.

      Further research into the causes of Down's Syndrome, the effectiveness of institutionalization, and the development of a number of educational programs (designed on the assumption that these children can, indeed, learn) have helped to point out the need for early educational opportunities for Down's Syndrome children (Hayden and Haring, 1974).

      Hayden and Haring cite a number of programs for Down's Syndrome children which have demonstrated the efficacy of early education. The Sonoma State Hospital in California, for example, conducted a highly successful language stimulation program with five year old Down's Syndrome children. Hayden and Haring report: "by 1967, the children were ready to begin a reading program, and at their eight-year test, nine of the ten children were reading, with a comprehension average of 250 words each" (1974, p. 39; see also Rhodes, Gooch, Siegelman, Behrns, and Metzger, 1969; and Bayley, Rhodes, Gooch, and Marcus, 1971). The University of Minnesota Down's Syndrome program, which emphasized communication skills for very young children, reported (Rynders and Horrobin, 1972) greater increases in cognition and communication skills in experimental children as compared with control children (see also, MacDonald, Blott, Gordon, Spiegel, and Hartmann, 1974).

b. *Cultural-Familial Retardation.* Frost (1975) reports that most children who are labeled mildly retarded (I.Q. of 70-75) have no clear neurological problem. Environmental factors have been implicated as a probable cause of such retardation. It has been shown that low socio-economic status (SES) groups produce infants who run a high risk of demonstrating later learning problems. In fact, Frost states that over 75 percent of the children who are labeled mentally retarded come from low SES homes. Hewett and Forness (1974) agree that compensatory education must be offered to disadvantaged children to broaden their range of experience and their understanding of environment. Socially and economically disadvantaged children at the kindergarten (preschool) level may require help in overcoming "cultural limitations, short attention span, underdeveloped abstract thinking ability, and lack of motivation for school success" (Passow, 1963: cited in Hewett and Forness, 1974, p. 87). De Wing (1974) cites studies by Hess and Shipman (1965) indicating that communication between mother and child in culturally disadvantaged families is deficient in both the areas of precision and meaning. Gordon (1968) refers to the effect that the nature of home-based early language development has on thought and language patterns in the child's later life. An additional influencing variable in the interaction cited by Gordon is that of social class. Both Jensen (1967) and Frost (1975) suggest that learning problems stemming from environment may be remediated or prevented.

3. *Physically Handicapped.* Jones, Wenner, Toczek and Barrett (1962) state that "the nursery school has substantial support as a functioning, extended family environment [which is] significant and essential to many children with cerebral palsy" (p. 713). In a brief review of the literature concerning early education of cerebral palsied children, Jones et al., cite Berenberg, Byers and Meyer (1952) in reporting "the value of nursery schools for these children as a means of altering social environment, providing increased sensory motor experiences, and 'laying' the groundwork for the patient's optimum intellectual and emotional development" (1962, p. 714). Koch (1958) states, "it is generally agreed that the early treatment of children with cerebral palsy produces better long term results than treatment postponed until undesirable motor patterns and

habits have been established" (p. 329). His statement is based on a review by Gesell (1954).

Both Jones, et al., and Koch feel that certain ingredients should be a part of the nursery or pre-nursery program. The former advocates an approach that emphasizes "teaching rather than therapy, both for the benefit of the child and parents" (Jones et al., 1962, p. 717). It is feared that early therapeutic emphasis will engender a later preoccupation with physical competence. Factors of emotional well-being such as personality development should be brought into play with other educational and physical considerations. Koch clearly advocates the inclusion of emotional guidance resources both for the handicapped child and his parents.

Jones et al. (1962), Jones (in preparation for publication), and Koch (1958) present discussions and/or follow-up results of early educational programs for cerebral palsied children. These results help document the need for early educational experiences for physically handicapped children and expose areas in which further research is needed.

The need for such experience is not limited to cerebral palsy children; it should be extended to include those with other restricting physical handicaps. Wolinsky (1974) notes the need for research into the effect of sensory deprivation and perceptual distortion on a child's development. Such phenomena may result from physical handicaps or restrictions or from casts which hamper exploration of the physical environment and force dependence on auditory and visual channels. There are also, of course, negative emotional effects imposed on children by hospitalization.

4. *Hearing Impaired.* Simmons (1966) in a description of the parent-centered preschool efforts for deaf children at the Central Institute for the Deaf states: "parent guidance over a six-year interval has led to the empirical conclusion that . . . the early years, which constitute the optimal period, need to be exploited fully" (p. 205); "a deaf child can grow in language during the pre-nursery period" (p. 205).

   In a discussion of management procedures for handling the child who is deaf from birth, Downs (1971) speaks of the period of development from birth to age three as "the formative years that will ultimately shape the educational course the child must take by the age of three or four" (p. 224). She refers to the preschool years from ages three to six as "critical years . . . during which language is learned" and as "the most important years in the child's life for intellectual development" (p. 224).

Northcott (1973) states that she "believes it is the inherent right of every hearing-impaired infant to be enrolled in a public school program or in a facility under contract with the public schools at the time the diagnosis of hearing loss has first been established and the psychological needs of the parents are at a peak" (p. 455). Northcott further states (1971) that in addition to the training a young hearing-impaired child of two and one-half to three years of age receives at home from his parents, the child also needs the experience of participation in a nursery which would allow him to interact socially with hearing children.

5. *Visually Impaired.* Whitecraft cites Barraga in emphasizing "the primary importance of the range and variety of concrete experiences in early life for the visually handicapped child" (n.d., p. 1). He continues, "the visually handicapped child urgently needs motoric environmental interaction as a readiness base for mobility" (n.d., p. 7).

   Mayer (1974c) states that visual impairments may retard language development unless a child is offered ample opportunities to explore his environment using other sensory channels. She also cites the need for communication with the outside world through verbal input from others.

   A preschool program for visually impaired children and their parents is justifiable on the basis of the amount of counseling and guidance needed by the parents. The parents need support in the areas of accepting the child's disability, overcoming misconceptions about blindness, learning the sensible limitations of visual impairment, and planning proper educational opportunities for the child (Love, 1970).

6. *Emotionally Disturbed.* Love (1970) states: "today there is an increased awareness of the problems [of the emotionally disturbed, and the benefits of] early discovery and prevention of social and emotional maladjustments" (p. 113). Mayer (1974a) says, "preschool children are just beginning to learn about their feelings and how to handle them. If they are given proper assistance when they are young, they have a better chance for sound emotional development" (p. 28). [See also Mackie, Kvaraceus, and Williams, 1957.]

   Love refers to the emotionally disturbed child as "a child who has emotional problems that are serious enough to adversely affect his relationship to some aspect of his environment—his self concept and his interaction with his family, peers, school situations and/or community life" (1970, p. 115).

Early assistance to children with emotional disturbances should include parents. Love notes that even the most motivated parents often find it difficult to aid their children because of the many variables that affect their roles. For example, the characteristics of the child with emotional problems often affect the feelings of the parents in a negative way. A well developed preschool program which involves child intervention and parent participation eases family tensions and aids the parents in helping and understanding their child. Early intervention, in other words, which includes parents has been shown to be effective in remediating emotional difficulties.

7. *Learning Disabled.* Learning disabilities refer to difficulties with the psychological processes involved in using language in either its spoken or written form that are not attributable to a primary cause, such as mental retardation. Such difficulties may appear in the child's reading, thinking, talking, listening, arithmetic, or spelling skills (Wallace and McLoughlin, 1975). Although a preschool child may not have become actively involved in trying to demonstrate his skills in some of these areas, there still may be indications in the child's developmental picture that problems will be forthcoming with proper early intervention. Francis-Williams (1974) says, "even though there are considerable individual differences among children in their rate of development, wide discrepancies in the growth of abilities in the individual child are unusual and call for further investigation" (p. 27). Francis-Williams lists a number of types of performances in various areas which she feels are indicators that the child may exhibit a specific learning disability at a later time. For example, early indications of language problems include "(a) lack of clarity in speech even in communication with familiar teachers and children whom they regard as 'friends,' (b) clear speech articulation, but the failure to use language as a symbolic process and to integrate its use into the performance of other learning tasks" (1974, p. 73). Francis-Williams cites Bayley (1966) in stating, "between the years of two and three basic language, i.e., verbal communication and comprehension, is most crucial for mental growth" (1974, p. 102).

Preschool intervention programs can be a method of eliminating (or at least reducing the severity of) the appearance of later specific learning difficulties (Francis-Williams, 1974; Wallace and

McLoughlin, 1975; see also Mayer, 1974b). However, Francis-Williams and Wallace and McLoughlin have pointed out the dearth of programs for dealing with preschool children exhibiting the early symptoms of learning problems, particularly serious ones. Wallace and McLoughlin state, "the organization of alternative service delivery systems on a preschool basis is as important as the educational provisions suggested . . . for school-aged programming" (1975, p. 300).

8. *Multiply-Handicapped.* Steele (n.d.) cites the growing awareness among educators of the large number of children with multiple handicaps capable of drastically altering development. She fears that delaying early intervention might make guidance and habilitation impossible later on, while making more costly rehabilitation and remediation the only possible course. She suggests providing "an intensive and highly specialized intervention, of an educational nature, into the life space of these young children" (n.d., p. 3). Steele feels that there is a positive correlation between early identification of, and service delivery to, the multiply-handicapped child and the prognosis for later adjustment throughout development. This feeling is supported by Guldager (1974) who speaks for a particular group of multiply-handicapped children, the deaf-blind, when he states, "the earlier a deaf-blind child can be identified and given direction in skill development, the better" (p. 295).

G. What are some additional examples of successful projects in early education for the exceptional child?

1. *Milwaukee Project.* Unlike a number of studies and programs, the Milwaukee Project approached the problem of cultural-familial retardation (CFR) from a preventive rather than rehabilitative basis. The Project, which is located at the University of Wisconsin, seeks to prevent CFR "by attempting to rehabilitate the family . . . therefore . . . preventing retardation in the new offspring of these families" (Garber, 1975, pp. 3-4).

   The families and children participating in the longitudinal study came from an area of Milwaukee that makes up only about 2 percent of the city's population but supplies about 33 percent of the educable mentally retarded children identified in the city's schools (Garber and Heber, 1973). The program is comprehensive in that it offers help for the mother and the high risk child. An

Infant Stimulation Program, for children as young as three to six months, is included in the total program. Trained paraprofessionals work with the children, first in the home and later in a day care type facility. Garber (1975) states, "the general goal for the educational program was an environment and a set of experiences which would allow each child to develop to his potential intellectually, as well as socially, emotionally and physically" (p. 6).

Evaluation of the five-day-a-week, seven-hour-a-day program has been conducted from many perspectives: medical, developmental, educational. Preliminary results of the program's evaluation (Garber, 1975) offer a very dramatic picture of the differential performances of the experimental and control groups. Garber states:

> The present data in all areas of performance measured, clearly indicate a marked superiority for the experimental group. Any ultimate evaluation of course, must be based on the performance of these children as they move through the educational system. We are encouraged by the preliminary results of the experimental group who have completed first grade, but final interpretations will be put off until more of the group have reached this point (1975, p. 14).

2. *Abecedarian.* The Carolina Abecedarian Project is a multidisciplinary longitudinal program conducted by the Frank Porter Graham Child Development Center at the University of North Carolina which was designed "to investigate issues in socio-cultural developmental retardation" (Ramey, Collier, Sparling, Loda, Campbell, Ingram, and Finklestein, 1974, p. 1). According to the project's objectives, this effort has a four-fold thrust:
   a. To demonstrate that socio-cultural retardation can be prevented through child-centered early education.
   b. To develop and evaluate an infant curriculum that can be used in a variety of educational settings.
   c. To discover which psychological and biological processes and mechanisms are affected by early intervention.
   d. To describe the relationships among psychological, biological, and family attributes during the first five years of a child's life (Ramey, Holmberg, Sparling, and Collier, in preparation for publication, pp. 1-2).

   The infants selected for participation in the project are considerably more at risk for later mental retardation as a result of social-economic variables than the general population. The infants are paired according to a number of environmental variables and randomly assigned to control or experimental groups. The experimental group receives day care services, including feeding and stimulation training, at the Frank Porter Graham Child Development Center while the control group does not. However, the control group receives a number of at-home advantages——such as free diaper service, infant formula and medical care——in order to control for nutritional health and other variables affecting the development of the two groups. The experimental group receives quality day care and a comprehensive stimulation program which is based on a curriculum of specific experiences and activities.

Assessments and investigations within the project take a number of forms. Included in the types of evaluations made are those of the curriculum itself, parental attitudes, home environment, and the biological, social and intellectual development taking place within the children.

Ramey et al. (1974) report that over 2,000 informational items are annually gathered on each child. The information ranges from intricate medical data to comprehensive family data. The project is attempting to identify the variables that affect development of the high risk child in a controlled fashion. Preliminary findings have shown significant differences in the performances of the experimental and control groups. Much more information is still to be gathered.

3. *Down's Syndrome Program.* The Experimental Education Unit of the University of Washington's Child Development and Mental Retardation Center has as one of its components a Down's Syndrome Program (Hayden and Haring, 1974). The project serves young children (birth through six years of age) with all types of Down's Syndrome diagnoses. The major objective of the educational program "is to promote the children's development of gross and fine motor, social, communication, cognitive, and self-help skills, so that their development more nearly approximates the sequential development of normal children" (p. 52). The children in the project have demonstrated gains in their skill competencies. The project is ongoing, which means more data is yet to be collected.

4. *Bricker's Project.* The Infant, Toddler and Preschool Research and Intervention Project (Bricker and Bricker, 1974; see also Bricker

and Bricker, 1971, 1972, 1973) was a non-categorical day care intervention program serving a variety of normal and handicapped children. The program's population included children displaying the characteristics of autism, hydrocephalia, cerebral palsy and Down's Syndrome as well as normally developing children. The program served children at different developmental stages, and from different socio-economic and ethnic backgrounds.

The project served as a research site: (1) for exploring alternative pathways for dealing with the young child; (2) for examining the question of proper assessment techniques for monitoring progress in early childhood education; (3) for developing a model for non-categorical placement of the young child; and (4) for offering a means for parents to be involved in their young child's education. The program placed emphasis on these four areas because the directors felt "that resolutions to these issues will provide some of the necessary information to formulate effective educational programs for the young at-risk or developmentally delayed children" (Bricker and Bricker, 1974, p. 4).

H. What is the extent of current state involvement in early childhood education?

According to Hobbs (1975), about one-half of the states offer some form of preschool academic experience for their children. In certain cases (e.g., Massachusetts and North Carolina), kindergarten programs have been made mandatory by legislation (Weber, 1970). At the time of the Hobbs' report, twelve states were authorized to serve handicapped children from the time of birth. Other states offer preschool educational experiences to their handicapped children beginning (depending on the state) between the ages of two and five. According to Hobbs, one state allows service at age two, two states at age three, four states at age four, and nine states by age five.

Ackerman and Moore report:

> . . . an analysis of the laws pertaining to preschool handicapped children by states indicates that in 1974 thirteen states had laws mandating provisions for handicapped children, thirty states had provisions for permissive legislation for preschool handicapped children, and eight states had no provisions for educational services for preschool handicapped children (the District of Columbia is included in these figures) (p. 11, in press).

These authors also report that most state preschool provisions are directed to the child above age three, with only about a third of the states providing services for infants.

The trend, as reported by Ackerman and Moore, appears to be moving slowly in the direction of mandatory educational services for handicapped children at the preschool level. Hobbs notes that there are a number of variables in how the services are offered which depend upon whether or not the programs are permissive or mandatory, the level of funding, and the entry ages of the children.

Hensley, Jones, and Cain (1975) report that over 70 percent of the states allow, through legislation, early education to be offered to handicapped children younger than school age. From 40 to 45 percent of the state legislation on preschool education is of a mandatory nature. Hensley et al. (pp. 47-48) have developed the proceeding graphic representation of state legislation for early education of the handicapped.

Early Education*

State	Type of Legislation	Compulsory School Age for Handicapped	Year Enacted
Alabama	Act 106**	6-21	1971
Alaska	CSHB 592, Ch. 79**	3-19	1974
Arizona	HB 2256, Ch. 181**	5-21	1973
Arkansas	SB 19, Act 102**	5-21	1973
California	AB 4040, Ch. 1532**	3-20	1974
Colorado	HB 1164**	5-21	1973
Connecticut	PA 627**	3-21	1966
Delaware	Permissive	6-17	1935
Florida	SB 89X, SB 77X**	5-18	1968
Georgia	Mandatory	Birth-21	1968
Hawaii	Act 29: Sect. 302021**	•Birth-20	1949
Idaho	SB 1362: Sect. 33-2002A**	6-21	1973
Illinois	HB 322 and HB 323	3-21	1972

State	Type of Legislation	Compulsory School Age for Handicapped	Year Enacted
Indiana	HB 1071, Ch. 396**	6-18	1969
Iowa	SF 1163**	5-21	1974
Kansas	HB 1672**	Birth-21	1974
Kentucky	KRS 157224**	6-21	1970
Louisiana	Act 306**	3-21	1972
Maine	HB 751**	5-21	1973
Maryland	SB 649, Ch. 359**	Birth-	1973
Massachusetts	HB 6148, Ch. 766**	3-21	1972
Michigan	PA 198**	Birth-25	1971
Minnesota	MS 12017**	5-21	1957
Mississippi	HB 74**	Birth-21	1973
Missouri	HB 474**	5-21	1973
Montana	BH 386**	6-21	1974
Nebraska	LB 403**	5-18	1973
Nevada	Permissive		1973
New Hampshire	RSA 186.A**	Birth-21	1971

State	Type of Legislation	Compulsory School Age for Handicapped	Year Enacted
New Jersey	Ch. 85, 178, 179 180 PL**	5-20	1954
New Mexico	SB 14, Ch. 95**	6-21	1972
New York	Sect. 4404**	5-21	1956
North Carolina	HB 1814, Ch. 1293**	Birth-20	1974
North Dakota	HB 1090**	6-20	1973
Ohio	SB 405 Mandate Planning Only	Birth-21	1973
Oklahoma	HB 1155, S13101**	4-21	1971
Oregon	HB 2244**	6-21	1973
Pennsylvania	Stat. 1371-72**	6-21	1955
Rhode Island	Ch. 24 Title XVI**	3-21	1952
South Carolina	Act 977**	6-21	1972
South Dakota	Act 108**	Birth-21	1972
Tennessee	HB 2053, Ch. 839**	4-21	1972
Texas	SB 230**	3-21	1969
Utah	HB 105, Sect. 58-18-1-10**	6-18	1969

State	Type of Legislation	Compulsory School Age for Handicapped	Year Enacted
Vermont	S98, Ch. 16, VSA 2941-2954***	Birth-21	1972
Virginia	SB 132 and HB 770**	2-21	1972
Washington	Ch. 28A.13**	6-20	1971
West Virginia	HB 1271**	5-23	1974
Wisconsin	SB 185**	3-21	1973
Wyoming	Ch. 15**	5-21	1969

*HACHE estimates based on personal communication with State Departments of Education

**Mandatory

***Permissive

Bibliography

Abeson, A. Movement and momentum: Government and the education of the handicapped. In S.A. Kirk and F.E. Lord (Eds.), *Exceptional children: Educational resources and perspectives.* Boston: Houghton Mifflin Company, 1974a.

Abeson, A. Movement and momentum: Government and the education of handicapped children - II. *Exceptional Children,* 1974b, *41,* 109-115.

Ackerman, P.R. and Moore, M.G. The delivery of educational services to preschool handicapped children in the United States. In T. Tjossem (Ed.), *Intervention strategies for high risk infants and young children.* Baltimore: University Park Press, in press.

Ausubel, D.P. How reversible are the cognitive and motivational effects of cultural deprivation? Implications for teaching the culturally deprived child. *Urban Education,* 1964, *1,* 16-38.

Bayley, N. *The two-year old.* Durham: Educational Improvement Programme, 1966.

Bayley, N., Rhodes, L., Gooch, B., and Marcus, M. Environmental factors in the development of institutionalized children. In J. Hellmuth (Ed.), *The exceptional infant* (Vol. II). New York: Brunner/Mazel, 1971.

Beach, F.A. The individual from conception to conceptualization. In J.F. Rosenblith and W. Allinsmith (Eds.), *The causes of behavior II.* Boston: Allyn and Bacon, 1966.

Bedger, J.E. Cost analysis in day care and head start. *Child Welfare,* 1974, *53,* 514-523.

Bereiter, C. Acceleration of intellectual development in early childhood: Final report, U.S. Department Health, Education and Welfare, Office of Education, Bureau of Research, June, 1967, Project No. 2129, Contract No. OE-4-10-008. ERIC ED 014332.

Berenberg, W., Byers, R.K., and Meyer E. Cerebral palsy symposium, cerebral palsy nursery schools. *Quarterly Review of Pediatrics,* 1952, *7,* 27-33.

Blank, M. Implicit assumptions underlying preschool intervention programs. *Journal of Social Issues,* 1970, *26,* 15-23.

Bloom, B. *Stability and change in human characteristics.* New York: John Wiley and Sons, Inc., 1964.

Bricker, D. and Bricker W. Toddler research and intervention project report year I. *IMRID Behavioral Science Monograph,* 1971, *20.*

Bricker, D. and Bricker, W. Toddler research and intervention project report year II. *IMRID Behavioral Science Monograph,* 1972, *21.*

Bricker, D. and Bricker, W. Toddler research and intervention project report year III. *IMRID Behavioral Science Monograph,* 1973, *23.*

Bricker W. and Bricker D. The infant, toddler and preschool research and intervention project. Paper presented at Early Intervention with High Risk Infants and Children Conference. University of North Carolina, Chapel Hill, May 5-8, 1974.

Bronfenbrenner, U. Socialization and social class through time and space. In E. Maccoby et al. (Eds.), *Readings in social psychology* (3rd ed.). New York: Holt, Rinehart, and Winston, Inc., 1958.

Caldwell, B.M. The rationale for early intervention. *Exceptional Children,* 1970, *36,* 717-726.

Caldwell, B.M. The importance of beginning early. In J. Jordan and R. Daily (Eds.), *Not all little wagons are red.* Arlington, Va.: The Council for Exceptional Children, 1973.

Carver, J.W. and Carver, W.E. *The family of the retarded child.* Syracuse: Syracuse University Press, 1972.

Coleman, J.S. *Equality of educational opportunity.* Washington, D.C.: US GPO, 1966.

Conley, R.W. *The economics of mental retardation.* Baltimore: The Johns Hopkins University Press, 1973.

Cooper, R.M. and Zubek, J.P. Effects of enriched and restricted early environments on the learning ability of bright and dull rats. *Canadian Journal of Psychology,* 1958, *12,* 159-164.

Dennis, W. Causes of retardation among institutional children: Iran. *Journal of Genetic Psychology,* 1960, *96,* 47-59.

Dennis, W. and Najarian, P. Infant development under environmental handicaps. *Psychological Monographs,* 1957, *71,* 1-13.

Deutsch, M. *The institute for developmental studies annual report and descriptive statement.* New York: New York University, 1962.

Deutsch, M. *Interim progress report, part II.* New York: Institute for developmental studies, New York University, 1968.

De Wing, K. Family influences on creativity: A review and discussion. In S.A. Kirk and F.E. Lord (Eds.), *Exceptional children: Educational resources and perspectives.* Boston: Houghton Mifflin Company, 1974.

Dowley, E.M. Perspectives on early childhood education. In R.H. Anderson and H.G. Shane (Eds.), *As the twig is bent.* Boston: Houghton Mifflin Company, 1971.

Downs, M.P. Overview of the management of the congenitally deaf child, symposium on congenital deafness. *Otolaryngologic Clinics of North America,* 1971, *4,* 223-226.

Ehlers, W.H. *Mothers of retarded children: How they feel, where they find help.* Springfield, Ill.: Charles C. Thomas, 1966.

Escalona, S.K. and Corman, H.H. The validation of Piaget's hypotheses concerning the development of sensorimotor intelligence: Methodological issues. Paper presented at biennial meeting of the Society for Research in Child Development, New York, March-April, 1967.

Farber, B. Effects of a severely mentally retarded child on family integration. *Monographs of the Society for Research in Child Development,* 1959, *24,* (Whole No. 71).

Forbes, L. Some psychiatric problems related to mental retardation. *American Journal of Mental Deficiency,* 1958, *62,* 637-641.

Francis-Williams, J. *Children with specific learning difficulties.* Oxford: Pergamon Press, 1974.

Frohreich, L.E. Costing programs for exceptional children: Dimensions and indices. *Exceptional Children,* 1973, *39,* 517-524.

Frost, J.L. At risk! *Childhood Education,* 1975, *51,* 299-304.

Garber, H.L. Prevention of mental retardation - The Milwaukee project. American Association on Mental Deficiency. Portland, Oregon, May, 1975.

Garber, H. and Heber, R. The Milwaukee project: Early intervention as a technique to prevent mental retardation. National Leadership Institute, Teacher Education/Early Childhood. The University of Connecticut. Technical Paper, Storrs, Connecticut, March, 1973.

Gesell, A. Cerebral palsy research and the preschool years. *Postgraduate Medicine,* 1954, *15,* 104.

Girardeau, F.L. Cultural-familial retardation. In N.R. Ellis (Ed.), *International review of research in mental retardation* (Vol. 5). New York: Academic Press, 1971.

Golden, M. and Birns, B. Social class and cognitive development in infancy. *Merrill-Palmer Quarterly,* 1968, *14,* 139-149.

Gordon, I. The young child: A new look. In J.L. Frost (Ed.), *Early childhood education rediscovered.* New York: Holt, Rinehart and Winston, Inc., 1968.

Gray, S.W. Selected longitudinal studies of compensatory education - A look from the inside. Paper written for symposium at the Annual Meeting of the American Psychological Association, 1969. Demonstration and Research Center for Early Education. John F. Kennedy Center for Research on Education and Human Development, George Peabody College for Teachers, Nashville, Tennessee.

Gray, S.W. and Klaus, R.A. The early training project: A seventh year report. John F. Kennedy Center for Research in Education and Human Development. George Peabody College for Teachers, Nashville, Tennessee, 1969.

Guldager, L. The deaf and blind: Their education and their needs. In S.A. Kirk and F.E. Lord (Eds.), *Exceptional children: Educational resources and perspectives.* Boston: Houghton Mifflin Company, 1974.

Hayden, A. and Haring, N. Programs for Down's Syndrome Children. Paper presented at Early Intervention with High Risk Infants and Young Children Conference. University of North Carolina, Chapel Hill, May 5-8, 1974.

Heber, R. and Dever, R. Research on education and habilitation of the mentally retarded. In H.C. Haywood (Ed.), *Social-cultural aspects of mental retardation.* New York: Appleton-Century Crofts, 1970.

Heber, R., Dever, R., and Conry, J. The influence of environmental and genetic variables on intellectual development. In H.J. Prehm, E. Hamerlynck, and J. Crosson (Eds.), *Behavioral research in mental retardation.* University of Oregon, 1968.

Hensley, G., Jones, C.D., and Cain, N.E. Questions and answers. The education of exceptional children. Report No. 73. Education Commission of the States, 300 Lincoln Tower, 1860 Lincoln Street, Denver, Colorado 80203, September, 1975.

Hertzig, M.E., Birch, H.G., Thomas, A., and Mendiz, O.A. Class and ethnic differences in the responsiveness of preschool children to cognitive demands. *Monographs of the Society for Research in Child Development,* 1968, *33,* No. 1.

Hess, R.D. and Shipman, V.C. Early experience and the socialization of cognitive modes in children. *Child Development,* 1965, *36,* 869-886.

Hewett, F.M. and Forness, S.R. *Education of exceptional learners.* Boston: Allyn and Bacon, Inc., 1974.

Hobbs, N. *The futures of children.* San Francisco: Jossey-Bass Publishers, 1975.

Hodges, W.L., McCandless, B.R., and Spicker, H.H. *Diagnostic teaching for preschool children.* Arlington, Virginia: The Council for Exceptional Children, 1971.

Hoffman, L.W. and Lippitt, R. The measurement of family life variables. In P. H. Massen (Ed.), *Handbook of research in child development.* New York: John Wiley and Sons, Inc., 1960.

Horowitz, F.D. and Paden, L.Y. The effectiveness of environmental intervention programs. In B.M. Caldwell and H.N. Riccuiti (Eds.), *Review of child development research (Vol. 3).* Chicago: University of Chicago Press, 1974, 331-402.

Hunt, J.McV. *Intelligence and experience.* New York: The Ronald Press Company, 1961.

Jacobs, J. *The search for help: A study of the retarded child in the community.* New York: Brunner/Mazel, 1969.

Jensen, A.R. Learning in the preschool years. In W.W. Hartup and N.L. Smothergill (Eds.), *The young child: Reviews of research.* Washington, D.C.: National Association for the Education of Young Children, 1967.

Jones, M.H. Intervention programs for children under 3 years. *TADS Infant Education Monograph.* Technical Assistance Development System, 500 NCNB Plaza, Chapel Hill, N.C., in preparation for publication.

Jones, M.H., Wenner, W.H., Toczek, A.M., and Barrett, M.L. Prenursery school program for children with cerebral palsy. Follow-up of 64 children. *Journal of the American Medical Women's Association,* 1962, *17,* 713-719.

Karnes, M.B., Teska, J.A., and Hodgins, A.S. The effects of four programs of classroom intervention on the intellectual and language development of 4-year-old disadvantaged children. *American Journal of Orthopsychiatry,* 1970, *40* (1).

Kirk, S.A. *Early education of the mentally retarded.* Urbana: University of Illinois Press, 1958.

Klaus, R.A. and Gray, S.W. The early training project for disadvantaged children: A report after five years. *Monographs of the Society for Research in Child Development,* 1968, *33* (4, Serial No. 120).

Koch, F.P. A nursery school for children with cerebral palsy: Five-year follow-up study of thirteen children. *Pediatrics,* 1958, *22,* 329-335.

Lillie, D.L. *Early childhood education: An individualized approach to developmental instruction.* Chicago: Science Research Associates, Inc., 1975.

Love, H.D. *Parental attitudes toward exceptional children.* Springfield, Illinois: Charles C. Thomas, 1970.

MacDonald, J.D., Blott, J.P., Gordon, K., Spiegel B., and Hartmann, M. An experimental parent-assisted treatment program for preschool language-delayed children. *Journal of Speech and Hearing Disorders,* 1974, *39,* 395-415.

Mackie, K.P., Kvaraceus, W.C., and Williams, H.M. *Teachers of children who are socially and emotionally maladjusted.* Washington: U.S. Office of Education, 1957.

Martin, E.W. Bureau of education for the handicapped commitment and program in early childhood education. *Exceptional Children,* 1971, *37.*

Martin, E. W., LaVor, M., Bryan, F., and Scheflin, R. Law review: P. L. 91-230, The Elementary and Secondary Education Act Amendments of 1969: Title VI, The Education of the Handicapped Act. *Exceptional Children,* 1970, *37,* 53-56.

Mayer, C.A. *Understanding young children: Emotional and behavioral development and disabilities.* Publications Office/IREC, College of Education, University of Illinois, 805 West Pennsylvania Avenue, Urbana, Illinois, 61801, Catalog No. 115, July, 1974a.

Mayer, C.A. *Understanding young children: Learning development and learning disabilities.* Publications Office/IREC, College of Education, University of Illinois, 805 West Pennsylvania Avenue, Urbana, Illinois, 61801, Catalog No. 116, July, 1974b.

Mayer, C.A. *Understanding young children: The handicapped child in the normal preschool class.* Publications Office/IREC, College of Education, University of Illinois, 805 West Pennsylvania Avenue, Urbana, Illinois, 61801, Catalog No. 114, July, 1974c.

Meier, G.W. Mental retardation in animals. In N.R. Ellis (Ed.), *International review of research in mental retardation* (Vol. 4), 1970.

Northcott, W.H. The integration of young deaf children into ordinary educational programs. *Exceptional Children,* 1971, *38* (1), 29-32.

Northcott, W.H. Implementing programs for young hearing impaired children. *Exceptional Children,* 1973, *40,* 455-463.

O'Connor, P.D. Efficacy of educational and medical intervention for prevention of mental retardation based on physiological and psychological research. *Australian Journal of Mental Retardation,* 1975.

Pasamanick, B. and Knoblock, H. Epidemiologic studies on the complication of pregnancy and birth process. In C. Caplan (Ed.), *Prevention of mental disorders in children.* New York: Basic Books, 1971.

Olshin, G.M. Model centers for preschool handicapped children - Year II. *Exceptional Children,* 1971, *37,* 665-669.

Passow, A.H. Education in depressed areas. In A.H. Passow (Ed.), *Education in depressed areas.* New York: Teachers College Press, 1963.

Ramey, C.T., Collier, A.M., Sparling J.J., Loda, F.A., Campbell, F.A., Ingram, D.L., and Finklestein, N. The Carolina Abecedarian Project: A longitudinal and multi-disciplinary approach to the prevention of developmental retardation. Unpublished paper. Frank Porter Graham Child Development Research Center, Chapel Hill, N.C., 1974.

Ramey, C.T., Holmberg, M.C., Sparling J.J., and Collier, A.M. An introduction to the Carolina Abecedarian Project. In *TADS Infant Education Monograph,* Technical Assistance Development System, 500 NCNB Plaza, Chapel Hill, N.C., in preparation for publication.

Rheingold, H.L. and Bayley, N. The later effects of an experimental modification of mothering. *Child Development,* 1959, *30,* 363-370.

Rhodes, L., Gooch, B., Siegelman, E.Y., Behrns, C.A., and Metzger, R. A language stimulation and reading program for severely retarded mongoloid children. A descriptive report. *California Mental Health Association Research Monograph No. 11.* Sacramento: State of California Dept. of Mental Hygiene, Bureau of Research, 1969.

Roos, P. Trends and issues in special education for the mentally retarded. In S.A. Kirk and F.E. Lord (Eds.), *Exceptional children: Educational resources and perspectives.* Boston: Houghton Mifflin Company, 1974.

Ross, S.L., DeYoung, H.G., and Cohen, J.S. Confrontation: Special education placement and the law. *Exceptional Children,* 1971, *38,* 5-12.

Rynders, J. and Horrobin, M. Enhancement of communication skill development in Down's Syndrome children through early intervention, Annual Report, Research, Development and Demonstration Center in Education of Handicapped Children. University of Minnesota, Minneapolis, 1972.

Sackett, G.P. Some persistent effects of different rearing conditions on preadult behavior of monkeys. *Journal of Comparative and Physiological Psychology,* 1967, *64,* 263-265.

Scriver, C.R. PKU and beyond: When do costs exceed benefits? *Pediatrics,* 1974, *54,* 616-619.

Simmons, A.A. Language growth for the pre-nursery deaf child. *The Volta Review,* 1966, *201-205.*

Skeels, H.M. A study of the effects of differential stimulation on mentally retarded children: A follow-up report. *American Journal of Mental Deficiency,* 1942, *46,* 340-350.

Skeels, H.M. Adult status of children with contrasting early life experiences: A follow-up study. *Monographs of the Society for Research in Child Development,* 1966, *31,* (39, Serial No. 105).

Skeels, H.M. and Dye, H.B. A study of the effects of differential stimulation on mentally retarded children. *Journal of Psycho-Asthenics,* 1938-1939, *44,* 114-136.

Smith, D.W. and Wilson, A.A. *The child with Down's Syndrome.* Philadelphia: W.B. Saunders, 1973.

Smith, M. and Bissell, J. Report analysis: The impact of head start. *Harvard Education Review,* 1970, *40,* 51-104.

Steele, N.W. The special purpose preschool for children with multiple disabilities. *The Distinguished Staff Training Monograph Series,* Vol. 1, No. 10. Program for Staff Training of Exemplary Early Childhood Centers for Handicapped Children, The University of Texas at Austin, no date, Bureau of Education for the Handicapped, U.S.O.E. Grant Project No. OEG-0-9-531306-(031).

Thompson, W.R. and Heron, W. The effects of restricting early experience on the problem-solving capacity of dogs. *Canadian Journal of Psychology,* 1954, *8,* 17-31.

Torrance, E.P. Broadening concepts of giftedness in the 70's. In S.A. Kirk and F.E. Lord (Eds.), *Exceptional children: Educational resources and perspectives.* Boston: Houghton Mifflin Company, 1974.

Wallace, G. and McLoughlin, J.A. *Learning disabilities: Concepts and characteristics.* Columbus, Ohio: Charles E. Merrill Publishing Company, 1975.

Weber, E. *Early childhood education: Perspectives on changes.* Worthington, Ohio: Charles A. Jones Publishing Company, 1970.

Weikart, D.P. Preschool programs: Preliminary findings. *The Journal of Special Education,* 1967, *1,* 163-181.

Weikart, D.P., Deloria, D.J., Lawser, S.A., and Wiegerink, R. Longitudinal results of the Ypsilanti Perry Preschool Project. High/Scope Educational Research Foundation, Ypsilanti, Michigan, August, 1970. Office of Education, U.S. Department of Health, Education, and Welfare Grant No. OE 4-10-085, Project No. 2494.

Weikart, D.P. Early childhood special education for intellectually subnormal and/or culturally different children. Paper prepared for the National Leadership Institute in Early Childhood Development in Washington, D.C., October, 1971. High/Scope Educational Research Foundation, Ypsilanti, Michigan.

Westinghouse Learning Corporation—Ohio University. The impact of Head Start: An evaluation of the effects of Head Start on children's cognitive and affective development, Executive Summary, June, 1969, U.S. Department of Health, Education, and Welfare, Office of Education, ERIC ED 036321, 1-11.

Whitecraft, C. Gross motor engrams: An important spatial learning modality for preschool visually handicapped children. *The Distinguished Staff Training Monograph Series,* Vol. I, No. 9. The University of Texas at Austin. Program for Staff Training of Exemplary Early Childhood Centers for Handicapped Children, Bureau of Education for the Handicapped Grant Project No. OEG-0-9. 531306-(031), no date.

Wolinsky, G. Current status and future needs in research on the orthopedically handicapped child. In S.A. Kirk and F.E. Lord (Eds.), *Exceptional children: Educational resources and perspectives.* Boston: Houghton Mifflin Company, 1974.

Zedler, E.Y. Public opinion and public education for the exceptional child—court decisions 1873-1950. In S.A. Kirk and F.E. Lord (Eds.), *Exceptional children: Educational resources and perspectives.* Boston: Houghton Mifflin Company, 1974.

Zigler, E. Familial mental retardation: A continuing dilemma. *Science,* 1967, *155,* 292-298.

Index